G000145022

Gillian Griffith

up the Creek without a Tadpole

*Dementia shatters and rebuilds the
bond between a mother and a daughter*

Gillian Griffith

up the Creek without a Tadpole

*Dementia shatters and rebuilds the
bond between a mother and a daughter*

MEREO
Cirencester

Mereo Books

1A The Wool Market Dyer Street Cirencester Gloucestershire GL7 2PR
An imprint of Memoirs Publishing www.mereobooks.com

Up The Creek Without a Tadpole: 978-1-86151-376-2

First published in Great Britain in 2014
by Mereo Books, an imprint of Memoirs Publishing

The address for Memoirs Publishing Group Limited can be found at
www.memoirspublishing.com

The Memoirs Publishing Group Ltd Reg. No. 7834348

The Memoirs Publishing Group supports both The Forest Stewardship Council® (FSC®) and
the PEFC® leading international forest-certification organisations. Our books carrying both the
FSC label and the PEFC® and are printed on FSC®-certified paper. FSC® is the only
forest-certification scheme supported by the leading environmental organisations including
Greenpeace. Our paper procurement policy can be found at
www.memoirspublishing.com/environment

Typeset in 12/18pt Bembo
by Wiltshire Associates Publisher Services Ltd.

Printed and bound in Great Britain by
Marston Book Services Limited, Ofordshire

Contents

Dedication

Acknowledgement

Introduction

For Rebecca and Bronwen

ACKNOWLEDGEMENTS

To the staff of Lamont Nursing Home (not its real name) for their outstanding care and love in looking after my mother. To Fran, Gil and Judy for their constructive advice and encouragement to just get on with it and to Olga, without whom it would never have been written.

I don't know why I come here
Knowing as I do
What you really think of me
What I really think of you.

- Leonard Cohen, The Land Of Plenty

INTRODUCTION

The challenge involved in caring for a demented loved one is well documented in the media, the press and in various autobiographies and memoirs. So why add to it, you may ask?

Because it is in the nature of our species to identify with each other. Every situation is different of course, but the fundamental problems are a common denominator. By sharing our stories we gain comfort or strength in drawing parallels, and there is always something to learn. Dementia is set to become a major health issue in the elderly in the next decade, so there is a need for us to learn fast. Some of us will become carers; many of us will become victims. It is a misconception that this condition affects only the elderly. Dementia drops like a pebble into the pond of family life and its ripples spread out in ever-increasing circles of devastation. Scientific declarations about cause and effect or magic pills are all well and good, but one thing is certain: we are going to need a body of information on how people cope or have coped. Individual stories allow people to connect with others similarly afflicted, if only on a spiritual level. The loneliness is assuaged for a while. One may heave a sigh of relief and say 'At least I don't have to cope with that'. Another may think, 'At least I am not the only one'.

When I started writing about my mother and me I didn't have a book in mind. She had already been in a nursing home for three months. She was happy and settled. I, on the other hand, was exhausted; still struggling with anger and guilt. I decided to become my own therapist and confront her through the written word. I started writing letters to her that she would never read, but as the words bounced back at me off the page magic happened. Without fear of censure I told it how it was for the first time ever and in so doing, released myself from her influence little by little until there was a book.

Some of my experiences will be common to many. One or two may be unique, provoke giggles or wry smiles. I found it was really helpful to keep one foot in the world of farce and comedy.

The sharing of stories promotes understanding. My own daughters told me that reading the words I had written had helped them to appreciate the enormity of the assignment I had undertaken, although it was tiny compared to that of some valiant souls who struggle on for years. It is so easy to sympathise with a bad day, a tiring day or a frustrating day; Granny being awkward again! But unless we promote an understanding of disintegrating relationships, the anger, the guilt, the helplessness, the feeling of treading water and trying not to drown, nothing will have changed when it is the turn of the next generation and we have become the victims.

My story flags up some of the perennial inadequacies in the mental health service and in the corporate care of the elderly and mentally infirm, which people in high places are finally beginning to acknowledge. But the demented don't have a voice. The rest of us have a collective responsibility to speak for them and to take some responsibility for our future selves. I was immensely fortunate to find a wonderful nursing home for my mother. We need to seek such homes out and sing their praises.

If this story prompts just a handful of people to set up an Enduring Power of Attorney in case it is needed, to name someone to speak for them if required or simply to accept that a hearing aid would be helpful, it will have made a small contribution towards an awareness of the problems ahead.

CHAPTER ONE

HISTORY

A year ago, when deep snow prevented me from travelling to see you, I wrote you a letter on your birthday. That letter opened a flood gate in me that had held back a torrent of unresolved emotions and questions.

The following reminiscences, of recent times spent with you, were not written sequentially, although they are presented in that way. They are plucked from memory much as a child may wander through a meadow gathering flowers as they catch its eye. The collected spray is a raggety bunch of short stems, long stems and some crushed stems that resisted the picking. But together they give the imagination freedom to conjure up a picture of the meadow and lodge a snapshot in the mind. By the same token, through remembered incidents and experiences, I have tried to create a snapshot encapsulating your descent into the chasm of dementia, through the troubled years between the death of my stepfather and your permanent relocation to a nursing home. During this journey my inner eye watches with interest, and records the changes that occur in me as I react to you hurtling back into my life, only to disappear again like a will-o-the-wisp.

Such transitions are difficult enough to navigate in ordinary families. Our family cannot lay claim to anything approaching ordinary. We are, and have been, a peculiar assortment of strangers flung together and held, or not, by the tenuous threads of matrimony. The enduring strand that remains between you and me, Olga, is a strand that has been stretched relentlessly from both ends over time. Our relationship has been fraught with difficulty since my teenage years, when you sabotaged the fragile connection between me and my father by introducing a man you told me would make 'a better daddy'. He did not. I disliked the later love of your life as, later, you disliked the love of mine. You and I tiptoed around each other in the ensuing years making conciliatory gestures, but the gaping fissures in our relationship prevailed. As I wrote, a curiosity surfaced from beneath the anguish, about the origins of our situation, and it drew me in.

I was an only child, born to you and William during the Second World War. I grew up docile, compliant and well mannered, a regular good girl. I learned from an early age never to upset or anger either of you, but I was rarely rewarded with any obvious show of affection. In this, your previous life, you and he were known as Babs and Bill. Your sister, Vera, who was less than pleased by your arrival when she was ten, called you

Babs on good days, disregarding your baptismal name, but on bad days you were 'the ugly bitch', on account of your pale skin and foxy hair. She, by contrast, was dark haired and olive skinned, like your mother.

Those two were already ten years into firm bonding by the time you put in an appearance. So you claimed that you were left to take your cues from your father, who was a canny and secretive man and a gambler, behind the locked doors of the Conservative Club. You adored him. He encouraged your independent nature. He became your confidant and even, in the face of your mother's indifference, arranged your first fitting for a bra, with a woman of his acquaintance. When he noticed your stride was becoming rather wide for a lady, he bought you a pair of high heels.

You were fourteen when you graduated from Miss Boden's School For Young Ladies and embarked on an apprenticeship with a hairdresser, also of your father's acquaintance. By the time you were seventeen you were fledged and fled from your home and your opprobrious sister to take up a job in North Wales.

You worked hard and played hard in the halcyon days before the war; times when wild young things went dancing and drinking and driving without a care in the world. Here you met Peter and captured his heart. You became the love of his life. He took you to meet his mother and then proposed. I am surmising here, but I fancy he was only one of the flowers in your meadow and your bouquet was still incomplete. You kept him dangling for several years and had the best of times. Then, just after war was declared, you announced your engagement to Bill, a gentleman, who appeared to be a man of some means.

Peter promptly enlisted, volunteered for bomb disposal and set off to get himself killed. But it was not to be. Instead he was mentioned in dispatches and honoured by the King. He returned from defusing bombs in Europe with a row of medals and a German bride.

Bill's war was less dramatic and much to your disappointment, he had no appetite for command or glory. You told me that he returned in 1946 much changed. He settled back into his old job in Liverpool, but he became quiet and morose, seeking out the company of 'the boys' in preference to that of his lovely wife and small daughter. To make matters worse, Bill's father's wealth, on which you had both had designs, was found after his sudden death to be greatly diminished, a precursor of further discord. You were bitterly disappointed. You had gambled and lost. You felt trapped and disillusioned.

When I was six we moved to a small town on the North Wales coast and a year later to another. We left a rented flat for a rented house. Then good fortune blessed you with a small inheritance which meant you could afford to buy a house of your own. It was a dream come true. But Bill procrastinated, finding fault with every property, and refused to commit, whilst constantly making demands for tranches of your money to augment his meagre salary.

Circumstances forced another move to yet another rented apartment, this time in a seventeenth-century mansion. It was isolated and baronial, which pleased my father, but you and I found it bleak and cold. Years later you revealed that you had given him an ultimatum: you would stay five years, until I was sixteen. You never disclosed what you had had in mind, or whether it was just an empty threat.

I was almost sixteen when Peter appeared at our door out of the blue. The German wife was history; a British passport had proved a higher priority than a husband. Peter said he had called to see your mother, who had given him our address and told him you would be pleased to see him. We will never know what else she told him. You were pleased, but the same could not be said of Bill or me.

Thus began a two-year liaison in which, in my naivety, I passively colluded. Two years during which you painted me one picture of your unhappiness and another of my father as a disturbed and bullying malcontent. Then one Monday morning you sped away in Peter's car, taking only a small case and your sewing machine, having never uttered a word of your intent. Your defection came six weeks after I began my nurse training. I had just been home for my first weekend leave. I wonder now if you presumed that I would second-guess your intention or whether I was simply a child raised and fledged, a job done, allowing you to move on.

You left my father a cursory note. His distress was awful. You never wrote or even spoke to me about your desertion and the disintegration of my home and family. Nor have you, ever. You just didn't see it that way. It was Peter who rang the nurses' home at the hospital to tell me you were with him. You reinvented yourself as Olga, with a new address, and gave yourself up to being adored. You were oblivious to my distress and contemptuous of my father's. It appeared that, from your point of view, the book was closed.

However, forty-five years on, there is a final chapter.

CHAPTER TWO

RELEASE

I received the message while I was on holiday in Spain. The doctor told me Peter's life was ebbing and they had run out of options. He told me he had been unable to make you understand that this time Peter was fighting a losing battle and he wanted your consent to discontinue treatment. He needed someone else to say what you could not. "Not me," I thought. "Please not me."

I had prepared for his death once before. He had told me himself that he was done, but he did not share his thoughts with you. The love you'd had, with its glitz and pizazz, could not deal with the truth that the glamour had finally gone. On that occasion, at the eleventh hour, they had found a way to mend him, giving you and me enough time to sink, unwitting, into the darkening waters of your dementia. My sporadic short visits had not warned me how close you were to disconnecting from your world, and Peter's pride had covered your tracks by keeping you so close by his side. Now suddenly you were out of reach.

In Spain, clinging to my daughter's phone, I heard the doctor say he wanted my consent to let your husband die. I corrected his assumption that I was Peter's daughter. The man had been no father to me, but he argued that as I was your next of kin the onus still lay with me.

I reeled from this disagreeable thought, but the doctor was pressing. He wanted an answer from me. As a nurse, I knew his deadly game; pitching the pounds and pence against the common sense that connects ineffectual drugs with impetuous souls. He said there were no magic potions left to save him, only the angels on the line. Peter was not my man but yours, Olga, and, as ever, you were 'in absentia'.

I released him for you down that wretched foreign phone. I agonised about whether I would ever have to justify it to you and, had you been capable, if you would have made the same decision. Then I made preparations to fly home.

CHAPTER THREE

REFLECTION

I said goodbye to my small family at the airport in Santiago, knowing it was likely to be some time before I would return. Tears finally overcame me as the plane soared out across the Bay of Biscay. I pressed my forehead against the tiny oval window, gazed unseeing at the vast expanse of water below and tried to remember the time when it had all gone wrong between us. Silent disapproval was your strategy when I failed to fulfil the dreams you had for me. I'd had no interest in a career in business, finance or law, where I might have met a 'suitable' husband. Nor had I any inclination to join an airline, where at the very least I might have found a pilot. Instead I decided to become a nurse, and you wrinkled your nose in displeasure, as I recall.

As soon as I was installed in a hospital you ran away with the man who would fulfil your dreams. You left my father and me with embers of anguish, and for a long time they burned holes in our lives.

Your disenchantment with me reached a peak when I

eventually married David, an artist, whom I had known since we were at school together. You and Peter criticised or mocked our every venture while you sailed together across the millpond of your lives. Now, all these years later, you need to be rescued, and the only name on the list is mine. Distance had become my breastplate and my only weapon, but you are about to be thrust into my care like an ancient foster child. We are mother and daughter, but we are as strangers and I don't know how we will make out.

I had been aware that Peter's health was failing, noted his pallor and breathlessness, his swollen feet and the bruises on his skin. But he kept your secret well concealed. By keeping me at the distance I had created, he protected you and preserved his own dignity, in some misguided way. He must have controlled the expanding gulf of your dementia within the orderliness of his own existence. I remember that I brought you some home-made soup and a cake one day and he admonished me for bringing food where there was plenty. But I watched you both consume it with the focus and pace of the hungry.

I knew I'd be wasting my breath to tackle the issue face to face, so I wrote a letter to you both asking you to consider making plans, while I was on holiday, for your future long-term care, bearing in mind that you were both already in your late eighties.

It was too late. You were in the arms of Fate already. When the phone call came, to say Peter lay on his deathbed, you and I had been awarded starring roles in a forthcoming dark and comic tragedy, and I knew that any future plans would have to be made by me.

CHAPTER FOUR

DEPARTURE

I made my way to the hospital soon after I arrived home. The room where Peter lay was bathed in spring sunshine. I waited by the door, contemplating the intravenous fluids dripping steadily into his arm and the oxygen mask dangling loosely by its pale green tube around his neck, while an Asian doctor completed a blood pressure check. Peter lay beached, blotchy and bloated. When he noticed me standing there, his eyebrows went up in surprise and he managed a 'Hello', but he rolled his eyes towards the doctor and back to me in a gesture that implied my collusion with his profound racial prejudice. No doubt you would have been amused, but I felt tainted and mortified that even in this desperate situation he scorned the hand that tended him because it didn't match his own.

The doctor smiled, and when I introduced myself he asked to speak to me before I left. A young nurse dashed in with ice cream in a bowl and handed me a spoon. "Would you mind?" she gushed, and was gone. Me, asked to feed the man who had never taken anything from anyone that he had not first demanded? Me, asked to nurture a man who, they had decided, was my responsibility, when he had consistently derided me and my family as incompetent fools?

I reminded myself that I was a nurse and picked up the spoon. However, the ice cream proved to be a step too far. His throat had already closed. After splutters and coughs, we came to an unspoken agreement and put it aside for never. I fixed the mask to his face and laid my hand on his swollen, lifeless one. I told him I would bring you to see him. He nodded and closed his eyes.

The doctor then confirmed what I already knew. Their treatment could do nothing more. Peter's blood pressure had fallen to the point of no return. I explained to him about you, that you were deaf, had refused a hearing aid and were beginning to lose your grip. I pledged my support for their care and signed the piece of paper that let him off the hook. Then I sat in my car in the bright April sun and considered how your life and mine were about to change.

I wondered how you would deal with the fact that Peter had reached the end of your road. I really had no idea. I was shocked by your dishevelled appearance when you opened your door, but was more troubled by your cheerful mood. You told me you were not quite sure where Peter was, but you thought he was quite probably up the road. I reminded you that he was in the hospital and said I would take you to see him. "Oh, he won't be bothered about seeing me," you said, "Not if he's got nurses to fuss."

"I think we should go anyway," I replied. You gave me one of your looks, which I read as, "and what do you know about it?"

I made you some tea and cheese on toast. I found you clean clothes, put your hairbrush in your hand and you in front of the mirror and then bundled you into my car clutching a small bag of Cadbury's Roses.

They had moved him to a small, quiet room. By this time he was unresponsive. He lay on one pillow, on his side, the way they had placed him. The air he breathed in, with effort, rattled ominously around his chest. You pronounced that he didn't look too good, but you didn't speak to him, even though I had told you that he would probably hear you. Nor did you touch him. You didn't hold his hand or stroke his brow to let his spirit know you were there. You placed the chocolates on the locker beside his bed. "No point in us staying here. We may as well go home," you said. The nurse assured you they would ring if there was any change.

It was a little after ten when the call finally came. You were about to go to bed. The nurse suggested we set off for the hospital right away, but you did not seem to appreciate that there was an urgency in her request. "You can go if you like. I never go anywhere at this time of night," you said. I was astounded by your refusal, but nothing I said could change your mind. You believed that the hospital was making a fuss. So I called a neighbour to sit with you and set off into the night on my own with your words ringing in my ears: "Give him a kiss from me".

The nurse who unlocked the door to the darkened ward looked surprised. "Is your mum not with you?" she asked, but she made no comment when I replied in the negative and made no excuse for you.

When I stepped into his room, a mantle of mortality seemed to settle around me like a shroud. The room had become a capsule of a life lived. All the boxes were ticked. Battles won and lost, people loved and lost. The music had stopped and the meter had run out.

Peter took his last breath within moments of my arrival. To all intents and purposes he died alone. I could not place the kiss you sent him. I was not the one he would have wanted to be there. But I sat with him for a while in the breathless room. Someone had placed flowers and a bible beside the bed. There was no sign of your chocolates. The dead have no need of chocolate.

Courageous, now that he could not answer back, I questioned him out loud as to why his anger had burned and what it had all been about. What did he gain from so readily scorning and spurning all who came close and keeping you all to himself? In that room he had so recently vacated, I admonished him for returning you to me, broken and all undone, and I admitted to myself that I did not know if I could raise the part of me that had died while I had stood in his shadow.

CHAPTER FIVE

REALISATION

My shoes squeaked on the newly-polished floors as I made my way back to my car through silent corridors. The black plastic bag containing Peter's few effects crackled in time with my steps. I passed an old man and a young woman clinging to each other outside the women's ward, bound together in grief. My eyes were dry. I felt nothing. The doorman eyed my black plastic bag and called out a sympathetic "goodnight love" as I negotiated the security doors out of the hospital for the third time that day.

Driving along black deserted roads, my thoughts tumbled backwards to a distant night and a previous, frantic journey to sit by the side of the cooling body of my father. He had not waited for me to say goodbye, but I had been there to comfort my stepmother. I remember that I telephoned you the next day to tell you of his demise, because we used to be a family. You were cool and abrupt. You sent his wife a bunch of flowers, but you spared no thought for me. This was years before you slipped into the cavern of dementia. I had put away the hurt, but it surfaced as I headed back to you that night.

The lights in your house shone like beacons in the darkened street as I pulled up in trepidation. Delivering bad news was not unfamiliar territory for me, but you were. I was anxious.

The neighbour opened the door. Her eyes posed the unspoken question and I shook my head. "He's dead" I said, and observed a single tear roll down her cheek. "How's Mum?"

Obviously perplexed, she replied, "Well, she seems quite cheerful really."

You came into the kitchen to greet me, as though for the first time that day. "Good Lord, I wasn't expecting you at this time of night. Is somebody dead?" It was clear that you had no recollection of where I had been or why.

"Peter died about an hour ago in the hospital," I said. I waited for your reaction. It came after a long pause, but it was not a wail or a rant or even a tear. Instead, you threw out a challenge, implying that I had told you a lie.

"Are you quite sure about this? There wasn't anything wrong with him. Those clowns at the hospital have probably messed up again. I think you'll find he'll be back in the morning when they chuck him out. They don't get rid of Peter that easily."

Nothing I said made any impact. You reinforced the invisible barrier between us and kept me at arm's length. No comfort was required. The ice queen was firmly in control.

Your neighbour stepped forward and took your hand. You looked quite surprised when she offered her condolences, to which you replied, "Yes, well. I'm sure it must be time you were getting home, Thank you for calling." The neighbour nodded to me and I thought I detected a hint of pity in her expression as she hurried thankfully away; whether it was for you or for me is anyone's guess.

After locking the door behind her, I turned to find you making a sandwich. "You must be starving after all that travelling," you said. And you were quite put out when I said I didn't want it. "Well I've made it now. So you'll have to have it for your breakfast instead."

I made some tea, wrapped up the sandwich you had abandoned and put it in the fridge. You followed me into the lounge and we sat opposite each other in the usual way. The events of the day had already retreated to the distant reaches of your mind.

I struggled to fathom the depths of your dislocation. How could you have sunk into such turbid waters without my knowing? I could not understand why Peter had not levelled with me about where you were heading. Now he was gone and my world shifted slightly on its axis as I discovered that chaos ruled in your head. I hoped that you were just in shock, and that by the morning reality might have reasserted itself

CHAPTER SIX

CONTRADICTION

You and I do not seem to be bound by the kind of love that is found between a mother and her daughter. Rather, we have stood, over time, as adversaries in an arena of mutual resentment. For years, we have skated around the edges of a frozen lake. The surface of it is littered with detritus from the fantasy bond we forged; birthday presents, Christmas presents and presents from abroad. But hidden in the murky depths lies a shared fury. We never spoke of love or hate or how we had hurt one another, or of how Peter had bewitched your soul and excluded me forever. Forever ended yesterday, and now you are adrift, no longer a wife but a widow.

I felt myself being sucked into the bedlam of your life as my own ordered world had floated away with Peter's final breath. For some reason, when I had thought about this scenario, I had imagined you would be distressed or anxious. I had even imagined you bereft. Experience should have made me wiser. You were none of these. I was the one at a loss. By the time the new day dawned you had done what you always did. You had pulled the plug on the truth and reset your belief to a more appealing tale. Peter was in Iceland, Cologne or Bombay. For "Peter is dead", read "Peter has gone away".

There was of course the question of a funeral, and I could see there might be problems committing this man to the earth or the fire while he was away on a business trip. Your iron will was as strong as ever, but I had yet to discover the extent to which dementia had taken your reason and shredded it. As I tiptoed round you trying to get the measure of your mind, you trapped me, immobilised me, like a venomous spider, and once again I was your fearful child, masquerading as a rational and competent woman.

"Did Peter make a will?" I ventured.

"What has that to do with you?" you asked.

"We will need to locate it today."

"Whatever for?"

"Because he died last night."

You considered for a moment. "He wasn't ill. Did they mess up?"

I went over what had happened again but you drifted off, switched off, refilled the teapot and poured another cup of tea.

I tried again. "Did he say anything about his funeral? Is there anything particular we should do?"

"He's not afraid of death, you know. He faced it many times during the war." You wandered away into another room and gazed out of the window into the garden.

"Do you know where his will is?" I probed.

"Those greedy birds are waiting for their breakfast," you replied. You took an old-fashioned brown case from beside your chair, unlocked it with a small key on your watch bracelet and sat down with it on your lap. It appeared to be full of brown envelopes and papers. You quietly sorted through them. I thought you might be about to produce a copy of the will, but no. After a while you locked it again and returned your attention to the birds.

I am sure he would have laughed at my futile attempts to convince you of reality. He would have scorned my ineptitude in the face of your opposition to closing the book on his life.

An unsigned will finally came to light in his trouser pocket when I emptied the plastic bag they had given me at the hospital, so it would appear that he had been considering his mortality. But it contained no agenda for his final jaunt. Had he gambled with the Grim Reaper one last time and lost? Or was it just the ultimate taunt from a man whose preferred riposte was "Don't ask me. Find out!"

I contacted the solicitor, who told me the will was only a draft and that Peter had never got back to him. He hinted that there had been a dispute of some sort with a previous firm, but had no idea of the name. I asked you, and you vehemently asserted again that it had nothing to do with me. I resorted to the address book in search of clues, and by a process of elimination discovered where the signed will was lodged. But of course they would not divulge any information to me over the telephone and gave us an appointment for the next week, when all would be revealed. I did however manage to persuade them to look at it and let me know if there were any indications of Peter's wishes regarding his funeral which would have to be arranged in the interim. There were none.

I came upon you later that day with your brown case open on your lap, like a child with a treasured possession. Over and over your fingers flicked through pieces of paper, and kept returning to one. It was a hand-written sheet that held your attention. You glared at me when I enquired about it and purposefully locked it away as though you were guarding a secret. I told you that the funeral director would be coming to see you the next day and would ask you about Peter's last requests and the arrangements for his funeral.

"Are you saying that he is dead? And if he is, why hasn't anyone informed me?"

"I informed you."

"How do you know, when I haven't been informed?"

"I was there, Mum, when he died."

"Well no one has told me."

If you were aware of his wishes, you could not, or would not, divulge them to me.

The funeral director, unaware of your mental state, was somewhat bemused as you cheerfully went through the details of a fantasy funeral. You agreed with his suggestions for a hymn and a psalm, but there were to be no notices in the press. "Good Lord, no. He wouldn't want all and sundry to know he was dead!" No wake or funeral tea. You couldn't stand parties. Lots of pink carnations would be nice. They were your favourite flowers. No church, no choir and no bell.

"That place up the road. Oh, what is it called?"

"The crematorium?"

"Yes. That will do very well."

You were not very interested in music. I said I would sort something out. You put on a really good show. You as the central character. You on centre stage. You as director and producer. Peter? Just an extra in the cast.

The business concluded, the funeral director shook your hand and reiterated his condolences.

"He's dead, you say? Hmm. Well that is as maybe. Thank you so much for coming. Will we be seeing you again?"

"It will be next Tuesday, as we arranged. The car will be here at one."

"Oh, quite soon then... lovely, I shall look forward to that."

CHAPTER SEVEN

CREMATION

The coffin rolls silently, on its shiny chrome trolley, to the front of the chapel, and we slide into our seats beside it. The large wreath of pink carnations resting along its top looks out of keeping with a military man. Red or white would have suited him better. The strains of *Morning* from *Peer Gynt* are fading when you nudge me and say, "Who is in there? Is it Peter?" It is your first and only acknowledgment that he may indeed be dead.

We had waited in the crematorium gardens for almost half an hour. Black limousines were stacked like deadly aircraft awaiting their turn on a runway. Grieving relatives strolled past our car from further ahead in the queue, sucking desperately on cigarettes and clutching mobile phones to their ears. Tidy men in shiny black suits stood about consulting their watches and each other with increasing concern. We learned that the clergyman engaged for the preceding committal had failed to put in an appearance. Municipal efficiency had been stopped in its tracks by a forgetful priest.

Our small group sat silently in the car, struggling with impatience and the fact that some of us had met for the first time that morning. Never one to tolerate a silence for long, you surprised us with, "Peter would be hopping mad if he was stuck in this lot. He'd say 'bugger it' and go home." The tension broke in the car and we were reduced to hysterical giggling wrecks. Our driver looked in his mirror and shook his head at our inappropriate mirth. Then the funeral car purred into life and crept forward, in the wake of the hearse, as we attempted to regain sobriety and control.

The gathered mourners had been required to wait outside on this chilly April day. They looked pinched and tight-lipped as they filed into the chapel ahead of the coffin and our small cortege; just you and me, my elder daughter and my husband, David, followed by Peter's two nephews and their wives. Amongst the other mourners I recognised only two neighbours, two ex-employees and Donald, the office accountant. In the preceding days I had spoken to many people on the phone, flying blind with your address book in my hand. I had relied on word of mouth to spread the news of Peter's death locally, since you refused to sanction any notice in the press.

"What about his business associates?" I had asked. "Some of them might wish to come."

"I don't want to see the bloody Germans. Tell Donald he can look after them at the office."

Donald had acceded to your authority without comment,

other than to say he would inform them, meet them at the airport and take them to lunch afterwards. You were still resisting all my efforts to arrange any kind of wake. "No, I am not going to be stuck in some place with hordes of people for hours on end." It was becoming apparent that Peter's last parade was going to be a restrained and unremarkable affair.

On the Tuesday afternoon, as arranged, we committed his body to the fire in an 'off the shelf' kind of way. We sang the usual hymn, about help in ages past. We said the usual psalm, about green pastures and the Valley of Death. I had no idea whether Peter was a man of faith or not, but I wouldn't have been surprised if his spirit had been lurking in some corner of the chapel, waiting to see what kind of a hash we made of it, and tutting that his expectations for himself remained unknown.

You sat, dry eyed, beside me, as the clergyman, who didn't know any of us from Adam, read out the short eulogy I had prepared. I had struggled with words of praise for this ruthless businessman who had been honoured for his bravery during the war. I had tried to convey the love and devotion between you and him, whilst carefully avoiding references to the past and to me. I had assumed the respect and regard of his wider world, whether or not it were true, and had endeavoured to put his life into some kind of context for those who may have been puzzled by this enigmatic and difficult man.

Finally the purple velvet curtain glided around the coffin and it disappeared from view. The deed was done and we sent him on his way with a jolly hunting tune by Mozart. Why hunting? Well, you said he was nuts about horses and without any other suggestions, the rousing horns had seemed a reasonable choice.

In the absence of a funeral feast, there was no reason for anyone to linger beyond the customary ritual of condolences and most people hurried away, already late for their next thing and peeved about the lack of a free lunch. The remaining few, business acquaintances, old colleagues and especially the Germans, looked taken aback and had difficulty rearranging their expressions when you greeted them with a cheerful smile, positively oozing charm. "Peter will be so sorry to have missed you. He is stuck up at the hospital at the moment but I'm sure he won't be very long. Can you hang on until he gets back?"

CHAPTER EIGHT

CONVOLUTION

"I don't see what this has to do with you."

I had just asked you about your gas bill. The final demand for the exorbitant cost of keeping you warm had come to light, secreted between the pages of a catalogue offering sheepskin products. I had been doing the one hundred and forty mile round trip twice a week for about a month by this time in an attempt to discover whether or not you could cope alone. Every other suggestion I had made had been met with opposition, based on the fact that Peter would not know where you were if you left the house. You tried my patience to the extreme.

"You really do have to pay this," I said, "You need to write a cheque today."

"I don't have that kind of money," you retorted. "Have you seen how much it is for? It can go down to the office and they can pay it."

And so began again the now familiar ride on the carousel of confusion and denial.

"The office doesn't exist any more."

"What do you mean, doesn't exist?"

"Peter closed it before he died."

"What about all the girls?"

"They all went on to new jobs."

"Why didn't anyone tell me?"

"They did, you just don't remember."

"Peter will have something to say about this when he gets back."

"You still have to write that cheque today."

"There may not be enough money in the account to cover it."

"There is enough."

"How do you know that? It has nothing to do with you."

The newsagent's bill emerged a few days later. That also was quite a sum, for five weeks of the *Daily Mail*, the *Mail on Sunday* and two local papers. You had hidden it beneath the tablecloth. I found it when I came to put a clean one on.

"That's not mine," you said, when I showed it to you. "I don't have all those and half the time they don't deliver them anyway."

I pointed to the pile of papers on the worktop in the kitchen and picked one up. The date was the previous day. "You still have to pay the bill."

"I think you'll find that Peter will have paid it on his way to the office."

"The office doesn't exist any more. Peter closed it before he died."

"Well no one told me."

And round we went again. There was no sign of a bill for the electricity, the water rates or the council tax. I searched the house each week, but you had become ever more secretive and your hiding places ever more inventive.

One day, while looking for the third set of keys you had hidden, for safety, and lost, I found the electricity bill. It was folded into a tiny square, concealed in an antique jar beneath a marble egg and a half-eaten chocolate bar. The council tax bill turned up wrapped in a paper napkin, inside a polythene bag, tucked into an old birthday card and neatly tied with green ribbon. It felt as though you were doing it on purpose to thwart me, although reason told me you were not.

When I had regained my equilibrium, I tried to persuade you to set up direct debits for all your bills, but I was wasting my breath. "Certainly not" you said. "Banks are full of rogues and thieves, and why on earth are you so worked up about it? It's not your concern. All the bills go down to the office."

"The office doesn't exist any more. Peter closed it before he died."

"Rubbish!"

The bill for the water rates never appeared. I rang the council to explain the predicament, but I came up against the Data Protection Act, which prevented anyone from discussing anything with me.

"Can't you put your mother on the phone?"

"No. She is deaf and demented. She won't hear you and can't understand."

"Then I am sorry, there is nothing we can do."

I was faced with the same response wherever I went. On a day when I was feeling bold, I broached the subject of Power of Attorney. You didn't seem to understand about it, although I knew you had once. I trod carefully, aware that I was on treacherous ground.

"It would mean that I could help you while Peter is… away," I said. "It might be a good idea to have a plan in case you are unwell or unable to get to the bank for any reason. A bit like an insurance policy you could fall back on."

"I've got quite enough of those thank you and if I need anything one of the girls will always come up from the office."

"Will you at least consider it? You can sign a paper to make it all legal and above board."

It was a good day. You acquiesced, and I saw my problems resolve. But when the papers came, you refused to sign them before Peter returned and they'd looked them over in the office. The carousel tune played again in my head. "The office doesn't exist any more. Peter closed it before he died."

"I haven't seen any papers to that effect. Nor have I seen a Death Certificate. No one has informed me of anything."

My patience snapped. I found the yellow form given out by the Registrar and handed it to you. "Read it," I said. "It states that he died. We cremated him. You were there!"

You gazed at the paper for several minutes, while I struggled to regain my control, and then you pronounced, "Well, that is as maybe, but I still don't see that it has anything to do with you."

CHAPTER NINE

CONSIGNMENT

"It has nothing to do with her. She knows nothing about anything." Your tone to the solicitor was derisory when she proposed communicating with me, rather than you, over the details of Peter's estate. I had spoken to her earlier about your failing mental acuity and she was of the opinion that you should be relieved of your obligations as executor when she realised that you were not up to the task, the fact that you refused to acknowledge that Peter was dead being the major impediment. In order to lessen the blow, she reasoned, "Your daughter is the obvious person to help you."

"I don't require any help. I am perfectly capable of attending to my own correspondence. If there is anything tricky it goes down to the office with Peter."

"My firm really would be happier if I could at least send copies to your daughter," the solicitor persisted.

"Well, if you must, I suppose you must," you finally conceded, "but I really don't see why you have to involve her."

When we finally walked out through the reception area towards the exit you turned to me, still on your high horse. "Well, I didn't think much of her. What a bossy thing! Who was she anyway?"

"She's a solicitor," I said, ushering you speedily out through the door.

"Not mine," you retorted. "She must be yours."

You secreted all the letters away, as I had predicted, and you refused to provide me with any of the information the solicitor required. I was forced to resort to subterfuge and raid your brown case while you were engaged with the mobile hairdresser in another part of the house. Fortunately you removed your watch, so I had access to the key.

In the course of this invasion of your privacy, I discovered the piece of paper on which Peter had written his last requests. They were scribbled, in pencil, at the bottom of a piece of file paper, beneath some business notes. Almost like a note to himself, or an afterthought. I had visions of you finding it and squirreling it away for safe keeping, but maybe you discussed it and he committed it to paper in a throwaway manner to appease you.

I breathed a sigh of relief when I read that he had wished to be cremated. I would have been dismayed if his preference had been for a plot in a country churchyard. It was bad enough to discover that you had thwarted his wish to 'provide any comers to my wake with meat and a drink or two at some local hostelry'. You had dismissed his lifelong devotion to you with a single word: 'No'. You had allowed the bomb disposal expert to simply peter out, and I had stood by while you did it. It was a significant measure of your enduring remote control over my behaviour that it took permission from a higher authority, the solicitor in this instance, for me to breach your defences and search for information that you withheld.

Notwithstanding my remorse about the funeral, I gained some strength and courage from this episode as I tried to build some structure around your life to keep you safe, planning my visits around your needs. As the weeks went by I became more and more aware of just how far you had retreated from the world. You continued to hide all letters and bills, and it was almost the summer before I discovered that the funeral director had been writing to you regularly requesting your instructions for Peter's ashes. Now mindful of his wishes, I raised the subject several times and was met with the usual resistance.

You never questioned how I knew that he had wanted to be returned to his birthplace in South Wales. I offered to take the casket myself, but you would not hear of it. I rang the nephews, who lived in Dyfed. He was their uncle, after all, but when they suggested driving up from South Wales to collect the casket, you thundered at me, "What the hell does it have to do with them?"

I wondered if you felt a reluctance to deal with this final separation and asked, "Would you prefer to have the casket back at the house where you can see it?"

"Good Lord no. He would never approve of that."

"Well he cannot sit on a shelf in the funeral parlour indefinitely," I replied. "By one means or another, Peter's ashes must be taken to South Wales. So what do you suggest?"

After a pause, you rose to my challenge with a solution that stunned me. "He likes parcels. He is always sending parcels. Tell them to send him in a brown paper parcel and tell them to send him first class by the fastest possible route. He'll enjoy that."

Wherever did this come from? Could it be dementia talking? It was certainly very black humour. You would not be deflected, nor engage in any more debate. I had asked you for a solution and you had provided it.

Thus, to the further amazement of the funeral director, the bomb disposal expert was confined within a brown paper parcel and consigned to his final resting place in double quick time in a van marked TNT. The nephews rang the next day to say the duty had been discharged. They had scattered his remains, by the light of the fading summer sun, beneath the beech tree he had planted as a boy, eighty summers before. The formalities all completed, he could now live on indefinitely in accordance with your sentiments.

CHAPTER TEN

ASSESSMENT

Over the years you and I have become distant relatives, by tacit, mutual consent. Now Fate has tied your only lifeline around my waist and I have been plucked out of my life and set down in the middle of yours. There is little common ground between us. We don't have any points of reference or notes for guidance. I am ashamed to find myself feeling irritated and resentful. It would be so much easier if we could talk together and sort things out together. I don't know how to help you if we cannot communicate. So I cast around for any other kind of help that might be on offer.

I started by speaking with your doctor. Could you be suffering from shock, I asked? He thought probably not. He told me your mind had been drifting for years. He had nothing to offer, bar one piece of advice gleaned from his experience with his own mother: "Whatever you do, don't uproot her from here and take her to live with you." I hadn't even considered that option.

He later wrote a report, ending it with, "She is coping well in her own home with the support of her daughter". He never once called to visit you to see for himself. I then asked a social worker to evaluate your situation. He came with boxes to tick and forms to fill, to rate the risk of doing nothing. To be fair, you were uncooperative and rude. You were convinced he was some kind of spy, sent by a nameless person and patently up to no good. You refused to accept an offer of hot meals, nor would you attend the local centre. You certainly wouldn't go for a walk or for a coffee and a chat – "Why on earth would I do that with someone I don't know from Adam? Haven't you folks got anything better to do?" you exclaimed. "I fail to understand why you are so interested in me all of a sudden. My husband will be back from Peru very soon and besides I have a daughter. Did you know that she is a nurse? In fact she is probably in league with you! So I'll go in the kitchen and make some tea so she can tell you some lies about me."

It was really a waste of his time, but he did suggest an emergency phone, a gas sensor and an extra smoke alarm, all of which he could arrange to have installed. He was pleased to have been able to tick three boxes and said he would make a report. When it came, it concluded, "She is coping well in her own home with the support of her daughter."

Finally, I asked the doctor to arrange for a psychiatric assessment. I needed to know where you were on the scale of 'going, going, gone'. The consultant who came to see you at home was a huge African man, wearing a tight, grey, silky suit. "Oh my God, he's black" you declared as he eased himself out of his car. I hadn't told you that he was a psychiatrist either. I feared you would insult or offend him, but you were very polite as you contradicted all the information I had previously given him.

"I'm afraid you are mistaken. I am not a widow. My husband is currently abroad. No, I don't live alone. My daughter is here, as you can see. Did you know she is a nurse? I wouldn't place too much store on what she tells you though. Of course I can get out and about. I can catch the bus on the corner over there. There's one there now, do you see? Do I cook? Well, I have something delicious for tea every night. I expect you do too. Lidl is just across the way, so it's very convenient. Oh yes, plenty of company. Too much sometimes. The girls from the office are always popping in for cups of tea and cake."

You thought you were being so canny as you spun the tale of your fantasy life. Your rules of exchange, with anyone in authority, are simple. Rule number one: beware of telling them exactly what they want to know. Rule number two: keep them guessing for as long as possible. Rule number three: if you are in a tight spot, find a way of evading the question.

The memory test was a problem; you did not know the day or the date. You offered the doctor the *Daily Mail* so he could check it out himself if it was so important to him. You knew your date of birth, but were decades adrift on your age. You could not remember the apple, the ball and the bicycle and repeat them when he asked you a few moments later. As for the Prime Minister's name: "Well, aren't they all the same and all as bad as each other?"

You could spell 'world' backwards, after a lifetime of doing crosswords, and you could recite your address. "Which county are we in?" he asked. You looked at me and pronounced with glee, "Not a hope in hell for us Gill, if he doesn't know which county he's in." Not in the least amused, he ticked the box that read 'Moderate Dementia'. He offered an expensive new pill that might, or might not, make a difference. He said he would arrange for some tests, X-ray your chest, scan your head and write a report for your doctor. When it came it read, "She seems to be coping well in her own home with the support of her daughter".

CHAPTER ELEVEN

MEDICATION

The hospital confirmed that you were indeed afflicted with moderately severe vascular dementia, but were otherwise in good health for your age. The magic medication that might improve your memory was duly dispensed and brought with it a host of other problems. Had the Mental Health Team been able to do joined-up thinking they might have realised that a woman with moderately severe memory loss might have some difficulty in taking a tablet at a regular time each day. It was highly unlikely that you would take it without prompting, and even if you did there was the distinct possibility that you'd forget you'd had it and take another or three. You had a similar problem with Cornflakes - one portion eaten and three in the bin, because you weren't hungry any more.

I was in two minds about the medication, Aricept. The indications said it was effective in mild to moderate dementia. You were classified as moderately severe, so at best you were on the cusp of its efficacy. However, on balance it seemed sensible to try it in spite of your objections.

"I don't need any pills. I never take pills. Peter's the one for pills. There isn't anything wrong with me, I haven't seen a doctor for years!"

Making the decision was easy. Implementing it was something else. I figured that if I engaged an agency to send a carer each evening, she could make you a cup of tea and a sandwich, make sure you took your pill and check that you were safe each night, thus relieving me of the worry that my once or twice weekly visits were inadequate. The service was too expensive for me to fund, so I had to consult your accountant, who had access to money specifically for your care. He agreed that it was a good idea.

You were not so easy to convince. You were vehemently opposed to any external interference in your life. "I might be out. Then they will have had a wasted journey. I don't want to be sitting here waiting for people."

"You never go out in the evening. You said Peter had told you not to."

"To hell with Peter, if I want to go out, I go out."

"It's unlikely that you'll want to go out in the evening, don't you think?"

"Well, I might decide to go to bed early and then they will disturb me. I certainly won't get up to let them in."

"What time do you usually go to bed? The plan is that they will come about five o'clock so they can help you prepare your tea."

"I go to bed whenever I feel like it, and I can sort out my own tea. There is always something delicious in the fridge."

"That aside, the most important thing is that they will remind you to take your pills."

"What pills? I don't need any pills. I can't afford to buy pills."

"You don't have to buy them. They are free. It's the NHS."

"Hmph! They won't be up to much then, will they? That lot didn't do Peter any favours, and what about these visiting folk? They'll want money, I expect."

"You needn't worry about that. Donald is going to sort it out."

"Donald? What the hell has it got to do with him? Peter will be hopping mad."

"Peter's dead, Mum."

"So you keep saying."

"Please will you just try it and see how it goes? I will be here on the first evening to explain your worries to the person that comes and make sure you get answers to your questions."

"Well, it appears I don't have any choice in this since you have already arranged it. I don't like it, and Peter won't like it either. I really don't think it's any of your business, Gill."

I had hoped that the same person would come most nights and build up some semblance of familiarity with you, even if you were unable to reciprocate. That was me still living in the world where joined-up thinking was the norm; where caring was a vocation, not a scramble to get as many people dealt with in the shortest possible time. We kept it up for nearly a year, but it could hardly have been called a success. I began to dread the five o'clock phone calls that came with increasing regularity.

"Your mum's in a panic. She says someone has taken her handbag. I've had a quick look but I can't locate it. Can I tell her you'll come tomorrow?"

"Your mum's lost her keys so she couldn't let me in this evening. Will you be coming tomorrow?"

"I had to climb in through the lounge window tonight. The keys are gone again."

"I couldn't give her a tablet because she has moved them out of the cupboard and we were unable to find them."

"Your mum won't answer the door. I've looked through all the downstairs windows. I can't see her. I'll try to call back a bit later."

"I think your mum's gone to bed. All the curtains are drawn."

After about three weeks I bought a key safe for outside and gave the agency the code. You hated the carers letting themselves in. Some of them complained that you were rude to them. Others just brushed it off or gave as good as they got. Several times you remembered that you could be in control, and bolted the doors from the inside. In short, the pills were a hiding to nowhere.

CHAPTER TWELVE

RESOLUTION

You have been living on your own for over two years. I have driven hundreds of miles to bring you soups, cottage pies, rice puddings, jellies and ham. Each week I have done your shopping. I have changed your clothes and washed your bedding. I have taken you out to visit the psychiatrist, the dentist and the optician. We've been to the bank, paid your bills and collected your pills. Several times we have been to the garden centre and had coffee and cheese on toast. I have placated your carers and bought you new clothes, since you have become so painfully thin. In spite of my efforts, you look bedraggled and grey, but your hostility towards me prevails. I dare not ask when you last had a wash, much less offer you any assistance.

You sometimes refer to having lovely hot baths. However, the resident spider, which I still haven't evicted, disputes your story and he is the one who laughs last.

I have tried to persuade you to consider some form of residential care; you would not even listen. You were angry and rude and appalled that I should even suggest such a thing. So we battled on until you forgot to care about the increasing hair that grew on your lip and your chin.

The dementia and I have been locked in a tussle since the day Peter died. He gave me only one clue to what lay ahead, and I missed it, when he made a throwaway remark in casual conversation: "If anything happens to me, you'll have to get her out of here right away." Did he really believe that I could bend your iron will, when you and he had spent a lifetime quenching my fire? Your mind may be cracked and fragmented and your short-term memory gone, but the programmes installed in your youth still played at the touch of a button; *The Secrecy Files, The Denial Tapes, The Fantasy Chronicles, Power and How to Retain It.*

I am reminded of a day, many years ago, when you and I visited your mother and found her cold, confused and hungry. Your sister had previously whisked her away to live with her in the south, but had soon brought her back when things didn't quite work out. You and Peter had come up with your own grand plan. You extended your house and built a granny flat for her, but by the time it was ready she was too far gone. The map of her world was reduced to the confines of her own small house. She had been unable to find your bathroom and she had peed on your chair, more than once. Like your sister, you sent her back.

On this particular day, long ago, I went in search of the District Nurse who came to look at your mother. She was no help at all. "There is nothing I can do," she said to you. "Your mum is not ill. She's demented. You will have to get a referral through the office."

Following her directions, we found the office in the nearby town. It was a mean and dingy place. The Social Services official, whose yellowing skin matched the nicotine bloom on the walls, was unmoved as we outlined the plight of your mother. In the days before boxes were ticked they were already well versed in the art of doing nothing. They had already learned to play the waiting game. We left the problem with him, but with only a vague hope that he might find a solution. He did not.

You phoned me a week or so later. Your mother had been found wandering outside in her nightdress and had been taken to the local asylum. You did not visit her very often. Your sister may have called once. A few months later you received a telephone call to say she had passed away. Forty years later we have turned full circle. The old lady is you, and I am struggling to keep you afloat. Your mind and your body are being ravaged by your indomitable spirit. The deadly mix of confusion and will is slowly cutting you off from the world. It may not be deliberate, but that's the way it feels when you thwart every effort I make to support you.

I leave a note stuck on the fridge to remind you that the pots inside contain food that I have prepared. The food goes off and I find the note in the bin. I place a small blackboard beside the sink, listing what I have put in the fridge, and you hide it under the stairs. I put a notebook beside your chair to remind you there is cake in the tin and I find it wrapped in a napkin, tied up tightly with string. You hide food around the house. I find things rotting or growing mould. You pour milk on your Cornflakes, then throw them outside, 'for the birds'. I warn you about cats and probably rats, but none of it changes a thing. When you can't find your key, you tip Cornflakes out through the window and the milk dribbles down the glass. Then you take me outside and show me the place where you say some toe-rag has thrown up all over your grass.

We could have continued like this until one of us fell over the cliff, but my family were not too keen on it being me. So it was with some misgiving that I booked a few days with my daughter in Spain. My preparations were careful and thorough. I stocked your fridge with things that you just might eat. I filled your purse with money, I spoke to your cleaner and told her my plans. I rang the surgery and left a contact number in ease of an emergency. I informed the care agency of the dates when I'd be away and I spoke to Social Services to make them aware that you would be flying solo for about a week.

I called on you on my way to the airport. You could not comprehend that I was going abroad, and I felt selfish and mean as I drove away. Through my rear window I saw you were at the door waving, but I knew I would be forgotten before you had turned the key.

The day before I returned, my husband called to say your cleaner had been in touch. She was agitated and indignant. You had apparently had diarrhoea on the bedroom floor and the bathroom was in a terrible state. She said it was not her job to clean up that kind of mess and she had left it for me to sort out. I understood, but I still felt angry leaving the airport and making straight for your house. Food and mould I could deal with. Unpaid bills and forgotten pills I could sort out, along with the rubbish in bags that you hid round the house and the flies that invaded the kitchen. I had spent a lifetime in attendance to people's bodily functions. It was part of the job to minimise fuss, faced with blood or vomit or excrement. For the first time I felt a revulsion, and I wasn't sure I had the stomach to deal with this, your most intimate decline.

It was almost lunchtime when I reached you, having stopped on the way to buy rubber gloves and sponges and bottled biological miracle. You were still in your night clothes and appeared quite distressed. The kitchen was all in a muddle. The milk was sour, the bread was stale and the food I had left had gone off. I was riddled with guilt for having given in to the need to replenish myself.

It was now glaringly obvious that no one would act to help you survive or keep you alive. You could not cope alone or stay in your home if deprived of support from your daughter. I got you dressed, went out for milk and made you tea and porridge. While you ate it, I cleaned the kitchen, before venturing upstairs with my gloves and a bowl of hot water. I soaked and scrubbed at the discoloured path that told the tale of your loss of control.

I was chuntering under my breath when you crept up behind me and made me jump.

"Is that shit?" you asked.

I looked up from my knees, "Yes, it is."

"What an awful mess. I had no idea. It must have been the children, I expect. You shouldn't have to do that. You'd think their mother would have sorted it out."

When all was returned to order and the house was clean enough to satisfy your cleaner, I scrambled you some eggs with toasty fingers and left you to eat them as I continued my journey home feeling disheartened and dishevelled and longing for a shower. My short holiday was in the distant past already. I was furious that the system fails in its duty of care. We do have to go to the edge and fall over before anything ever gets done.

I had to pull over into a lay-by as tears flowed for you and the disconnected daughter you had created. I wept for me, and my mother, a woman I sometimes hated. Then I pulled myself together and the miles increased between us.

At some point during the remainder of that journey, I decided we could not go on. I vowed to contact the Mental Health Team the very next day and tell them we were done. Whatever the process, it could start right away. I had played by your rules for two and a half years. The time had come for me to take control, regardless of what it cost.

CHAPTER THIRTEEN

IMPLEMENTATION

Several weeks after my decision that I was no longer prepared to be solely responsible for your safety and well-being, I was informed that arrangements were finally in place for your future care. In the interim, I'd had a long conversation with a new social worker and I was also interviewed by a different psychiatrist. I felt that their expectations were for me to prove to them that they should intervene, whereas my expectations were that they should make an objective professional assessment of what was in your best interest.

"I have been a district nurse for many years," I told them both. "I have initiated this kind of assessment and I know what I'm talking about. Just because I am Olga's daughter does not give you the right to question my opinion that unless I leave my family and move in with her, she is at risk. My twice-weekly visit and the minimal attention of very expensive carers is no longer sufficient. I am asking you to make that assessment and act on it."

The psychiatrist was very patronising. "Of course, I do appreciate that it has been difficult for you," he said.

"With respect, I don't think you have any idea how difficult it has been trying to run a family, hold down a job and be a long-distance carer for more than two years," I replied. He caved in and agreed that it was *probably* appropriate to look at the issue of residential care for you, even though you were absolutely opposed to it. He suggested a Guardianship Order, which would temporarily put you in the care of the local authority. They could then admit you to the nearby hospital for a detailed assessment and fairly swiftly transfer you to a suitable residential placement where you would be safe and well looked after.

They were soothing words which went some way towards assuaging the feelings of guilt that overwhelmed me. However, it transpired they were falsehoods, every one. I had been duped and, by association, so had you. Extracting you from your home became a monumental fiasco that would have had Peter spluttering venom into his gin. It was an operation so mismanaged that had it not been distressing, it would have been laughable.

Up to this point you and I had been real people with needs and feelings. As the mighty weight of the Mental Health Team lumbered towards your door we were transposed into the flotsam and jetsam of the caseload. We became 'incidental service users', ISUs, to be processed and have our boxes ticked.

The social worker telephoned me at six o'clock one

evening. "Just to let you know, we are going to move your mother tomorrow morning at eleven o'clock. It is imperative that you are there in case she refuses to open the door. There has been a slight change to the original plan, but it shouldn't present any problems."

I was taken aback by her abrupt tone and enquired, "What sort of change have you made?" She explained that there would be no Guardianship Order. Instead you would be subject to Section 3 of the Mental Health Act and detained for twenty-eight days at a hospital thirty miles further away than I had agreed, which would allow time for the hospital to assess your needs and for me to arrange appropriate long-term care for you.

"That is quite a significant change from my point of view," I told her. She was nonplussed. I was devastated. It was not how I wanted it to be. I could have said no. I could have changed my mind even at that late stage and we could have persevered to the end, but my courage failed. In a state of exhaustion and exasperation, I had selfishly given in to a glimpse of my old life. I should have realised it was an illusion. I fervently wished that an easier solution had presented itself, but an easy solution didn't exist.

My pulse was racing when I arrived at your house at ten o'clock the following morning. You were bleary eyed but, ironically on this day of all days, pleased to see me. I felt wretched as I bustled you through your breakfast and while you ate it, I quietly packed you a bag. I ushered you into the bathroom with instructions to wash. I sorted out clean clothes and brushed your hair, and all the while the clock was ticking. Eleven o'clock came and went, followed by the quarter and half hour.

From the window I could see the social worker standing by your gate. She was joined briefly by the psychiatrist, who then disappeared. She phoned me from the gate to say they couldn't come in without the doctor, but unfortunately the doctor had been called away.

By this time you were anxious. There were people loitering outside your gate. "Who are those people? Is there something going on?" I tried to distract you with coffee and cake, to no avail. "I think they are up to no good. You should go and investigate and tell them to go and do whatever it is somewhere else."

The trio of health professionals finally mustered just after one o'clock and walked towards the door. "Oh, Hell! God botherers. Don't let them in," you said. I opened the door and they filed in with mumbled greetings, but no apologies for being two hours late. Your house was suddenly full of people and you were overwhelmed. They introduced themselves to you and then, as if suddenly remembering that you were deaf, they propelled your doctor forward.

"You remember Doctor Radnock, Olga?"

You hadn't set eyes on him for over two years, but you pretended you knew who he was and offered them all cups of tea, which they declined. They sat themselves down in your lounge and the psychiatrist then went through a list of questions, drawing from you all the wrong answers, which ticked the boxes on the bright green form. Proof, if it were ever needed, that the correct decision had been made before professional witnesses.

I stood by the window and observed; not a witness or a nurse, just a daughter. You didn't seem to notice me. At first, like a fencer, you parried and thrusted. A dormant sensor in your brain was suddenly alert to a threat. In vain you attempted to foil all his statements, while digging a hole ever deeper at your feet. Finally you got angry and spat out, "I expect this is all Gill's doing. No doubt she put you up to this. Well, you can just clear out, the lot of you. I won't have you in my house. Go on, all of you. Clear out!"

You paced up and down in confusion, waving your arms about. You stopped lip reading, and I don't think you registered or understood anything more that was said. I stood by the window, in pieces. You still did not see me, and I dared not speak.

Then the interview ended. The allotted time had probably expired. The psychiatrist informed you that you were going to hospital for an assessment. You ignored him. He had already been dismissed. They all signed the green form and indicated the box for my signature as next of kin. I found my hand was shaking.

The deed was done, and they departed with unseemly haste. "Mark my words, my husband will have something to say about this when he gets back," you shouted after them as they hurried down the path. Turning to me, you asked. "Who were those clowns, and how on earth did they get in?"

There was a feeling of disquiet in the house after their departure. You and I were in limbo. A momentous decision had been taken. For all practical purposes nothing had changed, and yet, in reality, everything had. Judgement had been passed and you were no longer my responsibility. I had been demoted to short-term interim carer.

The enormity of what I had done hit me with force and I felt an overwhelming need to wash my hands. I was in a very lonely place. I telephoned my husband and he said, "It had to be done and there was no other way. Eventually it would have made you ill, and then where would we be?"

The social worker returned. It was almost two o' clock. She had arranged for an ambulance to take you to the hospital and it was expected quite soon, but considering your aggressive behaviour, she had requested a police presence. I argued with her that it was inappropriate, but she'd made up her mind. "She may be ninety-one and a mere five foot one but from her attitude this morning I'm assuming she'll put up a fight," she said.

"This is my mother you're talking about!"

"Quite so my dear, and as you are well aware, she is demented and unpredictable."

It was futile to continue. "Please, just get on with it," I said. "It is all taking too long."

I prepared you a sandwich and tried to explain to you that you had to go to hospital for some tests.

"What kind of tests? I don't know anything about any tests. There isn't anything wrong with me."You tied me in knots with your questions, and I squirmed like a fish caught on a hook. I still could not bring myself to tell you what I had done.

At four o'clock, the social worker rang again. The winter skies were already darkening. There had been an accident on the motorway so no police officers could be spared for an escort.

I zipped my lips in frustration. This day was beginning to feel like a month. I was tired, my nerves were at full stretch and my emotions had been through the mangle. We sat on and on, looking through your countless catalogues, as we often had.

At half past five the ambulance finally arrived. It backed into the drive, followed by a police car with blue lights and radios blaring. Two paramedics, in a blaze of green and yellow, came into the house wearing latex gloves and brandishing a copy of the psychiatrist's green form. The police came in close behind; a tall young constable backed up by his minder, a woman of twice his size, bulging out of her uniform through every available gap. Your personal space was invaded for the second time that day and I was astonished by your response in the face of this intrusion.

"How dare you walk into my house in the middle of the night! Have you been invited? Does my husband know you are here? No, I will not accompany you! I am not going anywhere. I never go out at night. I don't know you from Adam, and besides I must be here when Peter gets back. I don't give a fig about your bit of paper. You can wave it about as much as you like. No doctor has been here today and I am not ill. You can ask my daughter. Where is my daughter?"

I was curled up on the stairs in the hall. They told you you had no choice. The instructions on the form said you were obliged to go. You paced and shouted and raged. "I have not lived through a war only to be duped by yellow-bellied cowards that steal up on innocent folk in the night."

They were good at their job. I had to allow them that much. They manoeuvred you as far as the kitchen, and the policewoman blocked off the door. She began quietly asking about your life, your family, your husband. She calmed and soothed you. Then she suggested that you might just go for the assessment. She said it wouldn't take very long. She didn't actually tell any lies.

Suddenly remembering my presence, you asked "Where is Gill? What does she think?" I said that I thought you should do as the policewoman suggested. "These are busy people Mum, and the arrangements have already been made."

"Not with me they haven't. However, if you think it's all right…"

I helped you into your coat, wrapped a scarf round your neck and handed you the tweed trilby you always wore. They guided you as far as the open door. You looked out on the darkest of nights and changed your mind. "No! I'm not going. Peter would never approve. He has always said I mustn't go out at night."

One of the paramedics stepped outside and happened to look up at the roof of the porch. "Oh, there's a plaque up here," he said. "What's this? I can't quite see what it says. Can you see, Olga?"

"It's a cat," you said, stepping outside the door to show him, "and it says, "A very fine cat indeed". In the wink of an eye the second paramedic was by your side. They walked with you down the path, engaging you in conversation about all the cats you have never had. Then you climbed into the ambulance with the policewoman and never once looked back.

CHAPTER FOURTEEN

INTERMISSION

The silence sits heavily on my shoulders; I find it hard to breathe. I stand by the kitchen window and watch the ambulance disappear into the night behind the police car. Tears stream down my face.

The social worker returns briefly and places a hand on my arm. "Are you okay?" she enquires. And what if I'm not, I wonder. I stand by the kitchen window, transfixed.

"It's been a long, awful day and a long two and a half years" I tell her. She offers to make me a cup of tea.

"No thanks." I really just want her gone.

"Will you be going home shortly?" she goes on. I nod in reply. "I'll call you later then with the hospital details and the name of the ward so you can contact them." Then she leaves. Box ticked. Job done.

It is almost seven o'clock. I make myself a cup of tea and sit in your chair, in your sitting room, surrounded by all your treasured things. The china plates you have collected for years.

The crowd of teddy bears sitting, impassive, on top of the oak chest, orphans now. The knitting basket that had belonged to your mum. Your special nail file that doubled up as a letter opener. Possessions which until this moment defined you, spoke volumes about you, are now insignificant, soon to be forgotten, even by you. The house seems to deflate about my shoulders. Your haven of forty years has become a *Mary Celeste*.

The doorbell rings. It startles me and, for an instant, I think they have brought you back. But it is just the milkman collecting his weekly dues. I pay him, tell him you won't require any more milk and turn my thoughts towards practical matters. I need to go home, but your house will be empty and you have made a very public exit.

I wander through, checking and locking all the windows. I draw the curtains and pull out the plugs. I water your plants. Why did I do that? Your small brown case, containing all the evidence of your existence, I put into the boot of my car. In your bedroom I wrap up your jewellery and some silver odds and ends. I look in your wardrobe in case there is anything of value tucked away. Amongst the vast array of your clothes there are perfume bottles going back through the ages and several sets of Peter's false teeth. There are small bags of money from foreign places, fishing rods and Irish tweed hats, old cameras, silk shirts and a pair of dancing shoes taking a long break, enclosed in a polythene bag. At the back of a shelf I notice a small black patent leather case; like a box with the handle on the top. The fashionistas carried them in the sixties, but I couldn't imagine you carrying one anywhere, even in their heyday.

I place it on your bed and flick open the chunky brass catches, expecting to find scarves, gloves or perhaps jewellery that had fallen out of favour. The interior is lined with soft pink silk. It has retained the freshness of a summer rose, having never seen the light of day. The silken folds have settled around a dull brown leather case fastened with a thin buckled strap.

Inside the case I discover a heavy, cold and very real revolver. I can't tell if it is loaded or not. I drop it back into its incongruous hiding place as if it were a red-hot coal and close the lid. There is no sign of any ammunition. I wonder if you ever knew that this potent symbol of your husband was hidden amongst your frivolous bits and pieces. I don't feel that I can leave it here on its own, unsupervised, so I bundle it up with your jewellery and bury it deep in my car. My motives are honourable, but I still feel like a villain, looting spoils from the dead.

I pace from room to room, desperate to go home, but held by an invisible thread. I still feel a need to protect you and now an added need to atone for my betrayal. I am still angry and upset that you would not allow for a more civilized and equable solution. You challenged me at every turn. Your energy lay in the power of 'No' and 'Never give in'. Life's cruel twist was to tinker with your power of reason.

My victory, however, is hollow. I am relieved but far from jubilant, and I feel guilty even though I am certain that, if I had let you remain in your own home, things would eventually have gone horribly wrong.

I drive carefully. Not only because I'm tired and upset but also because I'm aware that I may have a lethal weapon stowed in the boot. At home, I hand my husband the shiny black case and tell him to hide it away in the barn until we work out what to do with it.

The Social Worker calls at half past nine to tell me you are 'safe and sound', and I reflect on her odd choice of words as applied to a woman so irretrievably lost.

CHAPTER FIFTEEN

HOSPITALISATION

November was living up to its reputation as the most dismal month of the year. The clouds hung low and periodically released their burden in torrential downpours. An increasing sense of dread overcame me as we approached the hospital. I had no idea what I was going to say to you, or what you might have to say to me.

I turned into the car park and the Victorian grey stone edifice of Middlefield General loomed in front of us, dwarfing its sprawling modern extensions with their familiar blue and white signs. Other people's visitors scurried inside out of the rain. I lingered in the car, gripped by the reality and consequences of my actions during the preceding two days. I had been over and over it in my head. Had I been too hasty in bringing down the woman who had dominated my life for more than sixty years? Had I been feeble in succumbing to anger, exasperation and fatigue? Was I heartless to hand you over to the Mental Health Team and relinquish my responsibility? An indisputable 'No' failed to present itself. I had hardly ever consciously angered you. It had been mostly by default. However I still feared the wrath you have never aimed directly at me but of which I have constantly been aware.

I had reluctantly agreed to my husband's offer of company, when he had valiantly said he would support me in what we both acknowledged would be a challenging visit, and I was thankful not to have to face this particular task alone. We braved the rain together and entered into the squeaky clean, cream and green reception area to ask for directions to your ward. A straight-faced clerk fired out, "It's straight ahead through the double doors, up the second set of stairs to the second floor. Go along the corridor through three sets of double doors and then turn left for Rollen Ward."

It seemed quite a hike. Visiting was at two o'clock. We had arrived early, so we made a diversion to the cafeteria for a cup of hospital tea. My cup shook in my hand, I was so anxious and apprehensive. I felt as though I was still in the middle of a nightmare, rather than experiencing a solution to one.

The minutes went by very slowly and we sat looking out at the rain until it was time to set off to find you. We strode along the shiny floors, our shoes squeaking with each step. We passed signs for 'Cardiac Unit', 'Respiratory Unit' and 'Children's Wards' and on past the 'Operating Suite', where made-up trolleys lay in wait outside. Was that the second or third set of double doors? Fellow visitors had peeled off along the way and we seemed to be the only people taking this particular route. We were clearly approaching the fringes of this antiseptic environment.

Finally we pushed through what we thought was the last set of doors. The temperature dropped, and an icy draught hurtled through a glass-covered walkway. The squeaky tiles gave way to a faded blue carpet. The windows were streaked by the rain and the paint on the sills was peeling and dusty. The walkway led to yet another set of double doors and another staircase, concrete and cold. At the top, the dark green doors of Rollen Ward came into view at the end of a dingy corridor.

There was a bell to ring for admission. We rang and waited. A nurse appeared on the other side, jangling a huge bunch of keys. I told her who were and that we had come to see Olga.

"Did you bring more clothes?" she barked.

"I've brought underwear, socks and pyjamas."

"Didn't they tell you about the clothes?" She looked exasperated as I shook my head. "You'll have to bring more clothes for her, a complete set for seven days. We will mark and launder them. She hasn't been seen by a dentist either. Her teeth are a disaster."

I was speechless in the face of this onslaught, but managed to mumble something about your refusal to comply with any treatment offered by your dentist. She ignored me, relocked the door and waved us ahead of her. "She's down there on the left."

Rollen Ward had the feel of a run-down community centre. Its decor was an all-pervading cream and green; smooth, shiny and wipeable. We turned in the direction the nurse had pointed and found ourselves at the entrance of a room about ten feet square, without a door. There was a huge television in one corner showing 'Flog It!' with the sound turned off. A motley group of old men and women were seated on plastic-covered chairs and sofas which lined three walls. Not one of them was watching the television.

I had a moment to study you with my trained eyes, ever a few takes ahead of the familial tie, before you noticed me. Your body was taut, alert, expectant, but your eyes revealed a complete disinterest in your surroundings. You might have been sitting in a waiting room or a hotel foyer.

When I approached you, you threw your hands in the air. "Oh, my prayers are answered! However did you find me?" and to no one in particular. "This is my daughter. My beautiful daughter, Gill." No one paid any attention. I brushed your cheek with mine and knelt on the floor in front of you, since there were no spare seats.

You noticed David behind me and greeted him with uncharacteristic warmth and cheer. Whatever I had been expecting, this was not it.

A nurse appeared and said there was room to sit down in another lounge. You introduced me to her too - "This is Gill, my beautiful daughter." The nurse commented on the resemblance between us and, as usual, I crossed my fingers and hoped the likeness was only skin deep.

The second lounge was cold. The chill November wind sneaked in through the bars outside the open window, a bleak reminder of where we were. I closed it. There were more cold green plastic chairs. The bare walls were painted a shiny hospital cream. On the top of an empty bookcase, which was fixed to the wall, was a plastic vase containing a dismal display of unseasonal plastic flowers. The only thing that could be said in favour of the ward so far was that it did not smell of urine.

A woman from the other lounge wandered in and sat close to us, trying to engage in conversation, but she had lost the art and she made no sense. When we didn't respond she got fed up and moved away.

You fired questions at me. "How did you find this place? I can't work it out. Is it near Chester? I don't know how I'm going to get home. Do you think there's a bus or a train? Have you seen Daddy? Does he know where I am?"

Before I could think of a reply, you turned to David. "I think I've messed up, David. I think I've really messed up. I'm right up the creek without a tadpole. I don't have any money to pay the bill either, but I would so like to go home to my little cottage. Can you get me home?"

He looked at me in desperation. How were we to answer you?

Before we had time to consider a response, we were interrupted by the sound of a woman wailing. It was a desperate, piercing utterance, which increased in volume as a small gaunt woman appeared in the doorway, supported by two nurses, her feet barely in contact with the floor. They tried to fold her into a chair, but she keened and went rigid in her despair. They made two more attempts to make her sit down before moving her on down the corridor.

We were both shaken by this episode, but you seemed quite unaffected and made no comment at all. This interruption had let me off the hook though, and you had quite forgotten all the questions you had asked.

We sat with you a little while longer. One of the nurses brought you tea in a plastic cup and offered you biscuits from a gigantic tin.

"Oh yes, I ordered these specially. You will put it all on the bill, won't you?" The nurse shrugged, indifferent, and moved on. You didn't mention the events of the previous day. It seemed that dementia had served both you and me well and had erased all memory of your ignominious departure from your home. In your muddled mind, I had turned up by chance, and only to help you extricate yourself from this mess you'd got yourself in. Again, I was amazed by your resilience. Your indomitable spirit was still plugged in. I had expected to find you angry, confused and indignant. I was wrong again. Your alternative reality had somehow transposed you from hell to a strange hotel, the only environment you had ever found comfortable outside of your home. You had become a detained guest and were behaving with your usual imperial dignity.

The charge nurse told me he found you amusing and had named you 'the Duchess'. I'm not sure you would find that amusing, and I guessed there would be other members of staff who would label you arrogant and haughty.

CHAPTER SIXTEEN

OUTFITTING

My new task was to provide you with seven complete sets of clothes. Although your wardrobes were laden with classic outfits and matching shoes, you possessed hardly anything that would withstand a thorough hospital wash. During your time with Peter you had become the undisputed cashmere queen and a long-time devotee of pure cotton and silk. During the last two years I had succeeded in passing off a few wash-and-wear items from M&S, but these were now past their best and it was clear that I would have to go shopping if I were to comply with the hospital's demands.

Everyone I spoke to said, "That is ridiculous. How on earth can people afford to do that?" My difficulty was not quantity but quality. I couldn't bear the thought of your beautiful things being reduced to dusters and dish rags. You were picky about off-the-peg clothes and besides, you were not going to be in that ghastly place for ever.

While I had looked after you, I had always paid attention to the styles and colours you preferred. As far as possible, I ensured that the image you presented to the world at large reflected who you were, who you had always been; in truth, a bit of a lady. It was with that still in mind that I set off to acquire indestructible clothes. So it was not surprising, therefore, that I discovered the odds were stacked against me. I couldn't buy red or lavender, lilac or puce. You had never worn white and avoided black – so dreary – and wouldn't consider anything pink. You didn't do patterns or 'shiny' and never wore silky unless it was silk. You didn't like low necks or V necks or polos and you hated bows, short sleeves and tight waists. You preferred shirts to blouses, rarely wore skirts and always had pockets in trousers. It is not a difficult undertaking to buy seven jumpers, seven pairs of trousers, assorted underwear, tops and socks, but I was handicapped by my enduring fear of failing to please.

After an hour or so of dithering, I took myself off like a fretful child for an espresso coffee and a bun. As I consumed the caffeine and carbs, I confronted myself with the reality. Since I could now guarantee you were safe and well fed, my problem was not you at all. It was me. For decades you had rented rooms in my head with permission to do as you pleased. You had permeated my thoughts, hijacked my every move. You had taken charge of my remote control and I had failed to wrestle it free. It was only when your mind became scrambled that I was able to generate enough power to override you.

Encouraged by the fact that the dynamics between us had

immutably changed, I set off again into the market place with renewed enthusiasm. There was no doubt that machine-washable clothes for old ladies were dire. You had never considered yourself to be an old lady when it came to buying clothes, nor had you ever been a woman with too much to do to fret about hand washing and dry cleaning. So although, of late, you had lost interest in your appearance, I could not bring myself to buy you a polyester frock, a flowery skirt or a lacy top.

Your mind might have gone into meltdown, but your body remains tidy and neat. Your hair still retains its foxy hue and you are dainty and light on your feet. Through all your confusion and muddle you had clung on to the remnants of style, and I recoiled at the prospect of your descent into a world without care. A world where, as long as it's clean and it almost fits, it matters not a jot what you wear. I determined that as far as I could, I would try to ensure that you looked 'altogether', even though you were not.

So I bypassed old ladies and focused on practical women instead. First up were acrylic jumpers, in terracotta and cream, beige and light green, camel, blue and coffee, then seven pairs of slacks, with pockets, in beige, brown and navy. I bought crop tops instead of bras, cotton pants, some passable shirts and two packs of socks for a fiver. In much less time than it took to swivel my mind, the cashmere queen was deposed. I had ticked all the boxes, spent over two hundred pounds and renamed you the Duchess of Acrylic and Viscose.

CHAPTER SEVENTEEN

COMPREHENSION

It is two days since my previous visit and I return to the ward with the bags of your new clothes. It is as dismal the second time as it was the first. The nurse who lets me in takes the bags. "Great, I'll go and mark them up," she says and scurries off down the corridor like a villain with swag. I catch myself wondering if you will like what I've bought, wondering if they will fit you; whether the trousers are too long. She is going to mark them anyway. There is no chance of you trying them on, and if they conform to your approximate size and shape and are marked with your name, they are what you will wear. She won't care.

I make my way through the cream and green to the lounge where you were before and find you, in the same chair, not watching another silent showing of 'Flog It!' I am dismayed by your appearance. It has taken them only forty-eight hours to transform you into a generic old dear, dressed in clothes left behind by someone else's mum. You are wearing a black velveteen skirt and a washed-out pink sweatshirt, several sizes too large and wrecked by the hospital laundry. Blue and white striped socks inch over the tops of your slippers but don't quite make it to your ankles. Your face is blotchy, as though it's been scrubbed, and your lips are cracked and dry. They have washed your hair and shaved your chin, but they have added a desperate caste to your eyes. I see my grandmother, all those years ago, as you sit clenching and unclenching your hands. For all my good intentions, I have fared no better than you. I have consigned my mother to the asylum, with twenty-five more days to go. I feel ashamed.

It takes a moment or two before you register my presence, but you smile with recognition and raise your hands in the air. "Hooray! It's Gill. I thought you'd never find me."

"I came the other day, so I knew where you were."

"Did you really? No one told me."

Your hands pluck incessantly at the pink sweatshirt. "I think this must be Vera's. It's too big for me. Looks like it's been washed by her, doesn't it? She was never good at laundry and besides, I don't wear pink."

"I think it really suits you. I've always said it would."

You consider the worn-out fabric for a moment or two and look at me over the top of your glasses. "I might have to shorten the sleeves," you say.

I had braced myself for a change in you once you entered that stark environment, but I hadn't factored in how much I would be affected by it. I found it very disconcerting that in such a short time you appeared to have lost touch with yourself.

The process had obviously been happening stealthily over some considerable time, but by keeping everything in place around you, both Peter and I had masked your inexorable decline. I was grateful for the element of compassion in dementia that soothes the victim when self-awareness fades, but it leaves carers like me in tatters. In a brief two days the hospital had pared your senility to the bone and in so doing had unearthed the long-standing sadness I have felt, that I, and my daughters, have missed out somehow in our dysfunctional relationships with you.

It had also magnified the shame I felt for having revealed the enormity of your undoing. I had known that your eventual exposure was inevitable, but the thought still irked that I had failed to breach your defences and come up with a more clement solution.

CHAPTER EIGHTEEN

DELIBERATION

The psychiatrist announced his decision after dallying for half of your allotted twenty-eight days. He labelled you elderly and mentally infirm, which came as no real surprise, but those three letters, EMI, effectively relegated you to the bottom of the residential care heap. Some small part of me had been hoping that even at this late stage, you could take another road. Your options and mine were now severely limited.

"Of course there is no way of knowing how long it will be before your mother reaches the end stage of dementia," he said. "It could be a year, two years, possibly five, depending on her general health. I would like to discharge her from here in two weeks' time so you can get her settled somewhere by Christmas. Do you have anywhere in mind?"

Naturally I had given it much thought, but the possibilities were considerably wider without the EMI connotation. Sensing my uncertainty, I am sure, he ploughed on before I'd formed my answer, "Does your mother have funds?" He was really asking whether you were rich.

"She has enough to live in reasonable comfort for the foreseeable future," I replied.

"There is a very good place not far from here, Sefton Grange. Do you know of it?"

I had heard of it. It was where professional footballers hid their demented grannies from the world. "It is set in lovely grounds and the care is of a very high standard, plenty of activities and so on. Good food of course, and it's exceedingly well run by qualified staff." He sang its praises so highly that I concluded that he probably owned it. I was sure it had plenty of style, commensurate with the exorbitant fees, but I couldn't see any good reason for you living a hundred miles away from me.

"I was really thinking it would be more convenient, for the family, to find somewhere nearer to where we live. My mother's connections in this part of the world are very tenuous."

"Sadly they will become tenuous wherever she is," he countered.

Family, of course, meant me. Your granddaughters and great-grandchildren had never had any significant place in your world but I believed, albeit fancifully, that if I could maintain that minimal contact, we might engender some semblance of a family.

"Well, good luck," he said and shook my hand. "You can always contact me again if you come unstuck."

I soon discovered that two weeks was no time at all in which to make such a major decision, and fell to wondering if the psychiatrist's delaying tactics were part of a cunning plan to fill the rooms in his exceedingly well-run residential home. He had left me just fourteen days to find you somewhere to spend the rest of your life and you, in the meantime, were adrift in the world like a sailing ship waiting for a favourable wind. In ditching one responsibility, I had acquired another. I wanted you to live the remainder of your life untroubled and in comfort if it were possible. The thought of you being confined to the doldrums of dementia, drugged or restrained by an EMI profiteer, filled me with dread.

I began my search by approaching all the homes I knew. None was able to take you. EMI beds were scarce. I heard of one a bit further afield and arranged to go on a visit. Then, by chance, I heard on the news that it belonged to a group that had been accused of ill-treating its residents. I promptly cancelled my visit and deleted the entire group from my search.

I scrolled through endless lists on my computer. I rang friends in the profession and asked for their advice. I waded through inspectors' reports, trying to read between the lines. Each time I found somewhere I thought might suit, the answer was always the same: "I'm sorry, we don't have any EMI beds at the moment."

It began to feel like a mission impossible and I wondered, for the millionth time, why you and Peter had not made a plan for the final years of your lives. Of course, in your fantasy world, people never became old, decrepit or demented, did they?

I discovered a converted country mansion which was not too far away. It was expensive, but they could offer you a place. I felt optimistic for the first time as I drove towards it in the winter sunshine, but on arrival I discovered that the main house was for gentlefolk of sound mind. The confused and demented were housed in a Nissen hut hidden away at the back.

The nurse who showed me round opened the door with an enormous key and the acrid smell of stale urine scalded the back of my throat as we went inside. The interior of the hut had the appearance of a seedy boarding house. The walls, doors and mopped floors were painted several shades of brown. The bedrooms were small and cell-like, all the windows wide open to the November chill. In a vast clinical space which the nurse called the day room, every resident was marooned in a reclining chair, fast asleep and well tucked in with a blanket. A single carer stood, like a sentry, beside a huge flat-screen TV with the sound turned down. The overpowering stench of urine had been unsuccessfully masked by disinfectant.

I was appalled and left, saying that I had another couple of places to consider. "Don't leave it too long," said the nurse. "The beds get snapped up very quickly." She seemed surprised that I hadn't booked you in straight away, but if it had been the last available place I would not have accepted it. I would rather have let you take your chance with the footballers' grannies.

I drove home saddened that my worst nightmare really did exist and that people paid huge sums of money in good faith to have their relatives looked after in such dismal circumstances.

I returned to the Yellow Pages, looked again at the small print ads, made another tentative list and was halfway down it when I came across The Lamont, an independent nursing home run by Daniel Lamont. When I contacted him he told me he had a single room available and asked me lots of questions about you.

"Why don't you pop over and see us?" he said. "You can have a look at the room and get the feel of the place, but I do suggest you come fairly soon."

I arranged to go the following day, encouraged that the inspectors had graded the home with three stars. The Lamont was a large house that had been built between the wars and had, at some point, acquired a sizeable extension.

Daniel Lamont met me at the door. He was a slight black man wearing a long white coat over a smart shirt and colourful tie. His broad smile was welcoming, and I could smell the beginnings of lunch wafting out from the kitchen. It smelled good. Several young people in pale blue tops were busy about their tasks. They also greeted me with friendly faces and cheerful smiles. The interior was warm and bright. A large Christmas tree took pride of place just inside the door.

"I've organised some coffee," said Daniel. "We'll go somewhere quiet and you can tell me Mum's story before I show you around."

Over coffee we discussed the financial details, the facilities they offered and the ethos underpinning their care. Daniel was a nurse and we discovered we had followed a similar career path, even in the same city at the same time.

"About three quarters of our residents suffer from dementia," he told me. "However I'm not in favour of using drugs to control it as they do in many places, and we are lucky to have a sympathetic GP. I aim to have higher staff-patient ratios, which allows us to manage problems effectively and the residents to maintain a quality of life for as long as they can."

It was exactly what I wanted to hear. There was nothing municipal or corporate about Lamont. It was essentially homely and comfortable. There were three separate sitting areas for the mixed groups of twenty-eight residents. The TV was on in one, the radio in another. Some people sat in an open walkway between the two, where they could watch the activities of the staff and speak to any visitors who came by. A canary sang in a cage by a window. A cat was curled up under a chair and a huge black sheepdog shadowed us on our tour, visiting each resident with a brief sniff as though checking his flock.

Daniel showed me the room that was free. It was bright and cheerful and he suggested you bring some of your own bits and pieces, to make it feel more like home, although it had everything you could possibly need. I had no doubts that Lamont would suit you and I felt sure you would be safe with Daniel in charge. My only worry was how you would react to the fact that he was black. You had always been racially prejudiced, but there were several black nurses at the hospital and you had accepted them without comment, so I prepared to take the risk that your fanciful nature would be taken by the name Lamont, and you would consider it suitably refined. It would not have pleased Peter at all, but I judged you would get value for your money and accepted the place for you.

Once I had made my decision, the arrangements were made with speed. Daniel went to visit you and within three days the psychiatrist had revoked the Section Order. You were no longer the State's responsibility.

They put you in an ambulance and sent you speeding towards Lamont Nursing Home. I received a telephone call from Daniel.

"She has arrived and everyone loves her already," he said. "I would happily look after a hundred old folk if they were as bright and amusing as Olga."

I concluded that you and he must have hit it off and my worries had been unfounded. "Only one small problem. She doesn't have very many clothes and nothing at all to sleep in. We can manage overnight, but could you bring some things for her tomorrow?"

I felt another shopping trip coming on and a letter of complaint to Middlefield General. It certainly explained how the hospital dealt with dressing patients whose relatives did not rush to provide seven complete outfits.

By the time I saw you the next day you were alert and chatty and back to your old self. You were tucking in to sponge pudding and custard when I arrived. "Did you make this? I'm sure it's the recipe I gave you. It's very good." The time you had spent in the hospital was completely erased. You were making a new start in a new little hotel.

"Peter and I came here before the war, you know. The place has hardly changed at all, I think the funny little chap that runs it is the same one as before. Peter will be tickled pink when I tell him."

CHAPTER NINETEEN

REDISTRIBUTION

You have been at Lamont for almost three months. Peter has been dead for three years. Nevertheless his presence remains in your house, contained in two wardrobes upstairs. There have been many times since he died when I have tried to suggest that we dispose of his clothes, and each time I have provoked the same response. "Are you trying to tell me he is dead? Are you saying that he is not coming back?" Each time I faced the same impasse. You refused to accept he was gone.

"He died. You went to his funeral and that's that."

You looked at me with derision. "Oh Gill, don't be an idiot. I am quite sure I would remember an important thing such as that."

Meanwhile, his clothes have remained in the wardrobes just as he left them, silently hanging to attention, awaiting orders which will never come. His cashmere coat is zipped into a bag with his dinner jacket and fancy white shirt. All his cleaned and polished shoes stand guard beneath jackets and suits and a blazer bearing the badge of the Royal Engineers. It was not until today, when I visited your empty house and opened the wardrobes wider, that I fully understood how well you had been drilled, by this officer and questionable gentleman, to be his surrogate batman over the years. The wardrobes revealed squadrons of shirts for every occasion, quiescent on the shelves. Warm Viyella, cool cotton and silk, long sleeves and short sleeves, country checks, business checks, stripes broad and pin, in colours of every hue have been impeccably laundered, folded and stacked, by you. Legions of sweaters relax in boxes and bags. Some have never been worn. All are made from the finest cashmere, merino or lambswool. There are blues and greys for the office, flamboyant yellows, mustards or greens for days off and diamond-patterned golfing styles, although I don't recall him ever playing golf. There are cabled whites for cricket. He had played for Glamorgan in his heyday, so perhaps he wore them on days out to the Oval or to watch the Ashes on TV.

Battalions of hand-knitted socks, all pressed and folded and colour coded, were billeted in a couple of drawers. Have you any idea how many pairs you must have made in forty years? Piles of white underwear line up on the shelves. Regiments of vests and pants in cotton and silk sit side by side with a ridiculous number of pairs of exclusive cotton pyjamas. From racks on the doors hang forty-six ties, twenty belts and pairs of braces. Twenty-three pairs of trousers stand by near the jackets and suits. In a cupboard above, hunkered down in boxes, I discover Peter's attachment of hats. A grey bowler, worn once on Concorde. A white stetson brought back from Arizona. A panama and a homburg keep company with several flat caps that match the Irish and Harris tweed jackets.

Peter's clothes paint a portrait of a vain and ostentatious man. He dressed himself and you for the world to see and admire. He planted his front garden each year with equal panache and proudly chauffeured you, out and about, in his low-slung Japanese car.

Even Peter, however, could not escape life's awful, levelling blows. I come across testimony to his decline in a plastic laundry basket, two pairs of jogging bottoms that had accommodated his distended belly, some polo shirts and machine-washable pullovers. A darker portrait, one that, even in your confusion, you had felt compelled to hide. Was it from yourself or from me?

I can still feel his energy surging through his clothes. They hold me in check, as he always did. I take a deep breath, recognising that I have to be ruthless and sweep him away as fast as I can and without thinking. I apportion all his clothes, hats and shoes into numerous black plastic bags, filling the back of my car, and distribute them among the various charity shops in the town. You would have been outraged by my disregard for his finery, but I am unrepentant. I hope there is a large man, from a bygone era, out there looking for a bargain, because today will be his lucky day.

CHAPTER TWENTY

CELEBRATION

It is your birthday. You are ninety-two today. I awake to silence and the luminous glare that signifies a fall of snow. In the garden, pots and bushes are iced, like fancy cakes on a damask cloth. The lane running alongside my house is smooth and glistening. There are no milk van tracks this morning. No one will be going anywhere today.

For once I had listened to the weather forecast and I had paid my visit to Lamont in good time, leaving your cards and presents with the nurses. I had pondered for days about your presents, not yet grasping the reality that they are no longer important. I had still adhered to the farce of writing cards in childlike script from your great-grandchildren so you would have more than just two, and one from your granddaughter in Spain, who has trouble keeping track of birthdays. I gave up reminding them all long ago. I had chosen your cards with care, searching for images of your favourite flowers, and it had crossed my mind that it was ridiculous to continue being tethered in this way. I had decided to buy you a pair of warm trousers with a check, a little bit sporty, and a leafy green jumper that would set off your auburn hair. It was acrylic, but it felt like cashmere and you no longer look at labels. I had wrapped each one separately and added gift tags from your granddaughters with their assumed love and good wishes. I had learned my 'kidology' from an expert.

'My' gift was a pair of cream faux leather machine-washable sandals. I envisaged the carers opening them with you this morning and bursting out laughing. "She must be mad, your daughter, sending sandals in weather like this." You won't be aware of the snow. You hardly ever go outside and you always loved new shoes.

Later, in the afternoon, I telephoned and they told me that you had laughed and clapped your hands when they brought you a cake with candles. They said you had sung Happy Birthday to yourself and then remarked that it must be somebody's birthday. Nevertheless you had blown out the candles with one puff and they had taken your photo and would print one for me to keep.

Stuck at home in the snow, I recalled your birthdays in years gone by. You liked to spread them over several days, never content with just one, and wherever I was, you expected me to pay you a visit. In the early years, when hostilities were suspended for a while, the children came too, bearing home-made cards and gifts. They knew they were expected to make you feel special, and they did their very best. You always prepared a feast with cold beef or cold ham and the earliest new potatoes. There was always a green salad with watercress and grapes, long before we all had green salad with everything. For dessert you made a sponge cake filled with fresh raspberries and cream, and Peter ate cold rice pudding because he couldn't stand the seeds getting stuck in his teeth.

Despite the occasion, the atmosphere eventually settled around us like an adhesive cloud that stuck us to our chairs. There was never a welcome from Peter, and he grumbled as he hoovered around us, removing crumbs from your dark green carpet, before banishing the children to TV Land in another room. Nevertheless, you held us fast and when we finally succeeded in driving away, it felt like an escape, but without the buzz that accompanies freedom. We always felt low and depleted, and sang silly songs and played games on the way home till we felt normal again. It was not until years later that I understood you had been surreptitiously syphoning off our energy, taking every last ounce to feed your own ego.

You won't know that today is your birthday. Your presents will be just some old things passed on by your sister. You won't be expecting a visit from your daughter. So why do I feel that I've failed again because the snow got in my way?

CHAPTER TWENTY ONE

FRUSTRATION

I am beginning to get accustomed to the idea that you will never return to your home. I am slowly coming to terms with the fact that it has become my responsibility to decide how to disperse your belongings and look after your house for the foreseeable future, but I am still consumed by the feelings I had that first night after you left. I still feel like a snooper and a thief. Little by little, with each consecutive visit, I try to assess the task ahead and come to some decisions. My weekly visits to Lamont serve only to increase my anxiety. We are in a state of limbo again. In many ways, and I find it hard to admit this, even to myself, your hold over me is so strong that I would find it easier if you had died.

Today I force myself to go into your bedroom with its identical twin beds, Peter's still made up, ready for his return. Your fitted wardrobes are as yet unexplored. I open one of the doors and sit down on the floor in front of it. The empty house sighs and creaks around me and I half expect you to appear at the door and ask me what on earth I think I am doing.

I have just removed half a dozen boxes of brand new shoes from the base of the wardrobe when my eye is caught by a small package that must have been secreted behind them. Its splash of turquoise blue shrieks into the silent array of autumn colours that hang above on sturdy wooden hangers. I stretch forward into the corner to reach it and discover that the wrapping is a piece of fabric. It is expertly folded and secured with twisted strips of polythene in lieu of string. Your mastery of knots, learned when you were in the Girl Guides, endured long after your ability to heat a pan of soup had deserted you. I struggle with the knots, hearing your voice in my head: "Be patient. Just sit with it. It will give."

I am impatient now, and polythene does not behave like string. I resort to the scissors from the bathroom cabinet and a silk scarf unfolds into a turquoise blue puddle in my lap, revealing a plastic bag firmly secured with scotch tape. Employing the scissors again, I release a right-handed black thermal glove. The scarf and the glove provide irrefutable evidence of dementia's reach in its meddling with the mind. You never, ever, wore black. It was altogether too dreary. Furthermore, auburn-haired into old age, and with a personal palette set in your youth, you would no more give turquoise blue the time of day than buy cheap underwear.

While I am puzzling over the provenance of these incongruous items, my fingers trace a small rectangular shape within the glove. A single shake reveals a small freezer bag crisscrossed with several elastic bands stretched and twisted tightly around its exterior. Each crossing place is neatly aligned with all the others. At this point my mind hurtles back through the decades to birthday parties in my childhood; to games of pass the parcel. Sitting on the floor in a circle, we dilly-dallied with the parcel as the music played, willing it to be in our hands when the music stopped. Excitement mounted with each cast-off layer, and there was a chance that the next one might deliver the prize.

No music plays as I ease off the elastic bands, open the freezer bag and remove a gold cardboard jewellery box, its corners scuffed with age. My heart skips a beat. I am certain I have seen this box before. I am equally certain it contains a single strand of tiny, blushing pearls wrapped in yellowing cotton wool. I'd been told they were brought across the South China Sea in a clipper ship by my great grandfather and given to his daughter-in-law, Edith, my grandmother. It is many years since I have seen this necklace. You were never a twin set and pearls girl, even in the fifties; especially in the fifties, when everyone wore pearls. You kept them tucked away with other items that Bill had bought but which you hadn't chosen for yourself.

I remove the lid of the box to find only a piece of scrunched-up newspaper. Anger flares; the little box is empty. I carefully spread out the small piece of newsprint so I can read it. Are you perhaps still playing games with me? Have you left me another clue?

The scrap of paper is torn from the small ads section of the local paper. "Sally's Secretarial Services. Fast, Efficient and Flexible."

No games, no clues and no pearls. Just bitter disappointment and heartache at yet another manifestation of the inexplicable deviations of a demented mind. I mourn the disappearance of my grandmother's pearls, but hold on to the idea that they may yet turn up in another unexpected guise.

Anger and sorrow having depleted my energy again, I close the wardrobe door and leave your house and its secrets for another day.

CHAPTER TWENTY TWO

RECOLLECTIONS

When I look into your wardrobes, I visualise a woman with style. A woman who is well versed in the art of looking good. A woman at ease with her foxy hair and peachy skin. Someone with the means to indulge her fancies and no need to compromise on quality or luxury; cashmere and silk in abundance, real leather and suede.

In the wardrobes, prestigious labels mingle freely. Burberry snuggles down with Windsmoor. Aquascutum jostles for space with Jaeger. An array of silk shirts coordinates with all the trousers and skirts. Soft woollen jumpers and jackets, from Scotland, nestle comfortably amongst camphor sachets and cedar wood balls. Drawers of vibrant silk scarves tumble around each other, a kaleidoscope of colour. Your hand-made shoes stack up neatly, still in their original boxes. Flat shoes, in every conceivable hue, are tightly packed in a communal wooden box. Lace-ups, moccasins and sandals suggest acceptance of advancing years; Padders and Hotter are far from prestigious. Two pairs of heeled and strappy shoes take a long break in a sealed polythene bag. Dancing days are over.

There are linen dresses from Ireland, tartan skirts and trews from north of the border, American cotton shirts and skirts and several exclusive suits from the Rhineland, all zipped into protective bags. Your coats occupy a whole wardrobe by themselves. It could never be said that you were inappropriately clad for season, occasion or weather. You have long coats, short coats and three-quarter coats. Pure wool and sheepskin for the winter; woollen blends and suede for the spring; linen and cotton for the summer. You don't much care for the heat, I recall. You have waxed coats, trench coats and pack-away coats to keep inclement weather at bay.

There are jackets and blazers for formal and informal occasions, wind-cheaters for the chilly decks of the river cruise ships and subtle green macs for fishing trips when you tagged along with your man. On their own, below stairs, in the hall, hang two Marks & Spencer anoraks, one thick and one thin, for winter and spring, exclusively worn for popping out shopping.

More drawers disclose a plethora of lambswool, cashmere and mohair scarves, along with a collection of hats and gloves; evidence of your abhorrence of draughts and the wind in your hair. There are soft leather gloves, a perfect match to all the hand-made shoes; driving gloves with leather palms and string backs; sheepskin gloves and sheepskin mittens; knitted gloves and gloves with thermal linings. There are knitted hats, sheepskin hats and felt hats and a genuine fur hat from Canada, carefully wrapped in a cotton cloth. Your favourite hats were trilbies made from

Irish tweed. It was your style of choice and you wore it long before Kate Moss teamed hers with micro shorts and set the fashion world alight.

Several months have elapsed since you were lured away from your home into the man-made world of Lamont. I have peeked into your wardrobe once or twice, but could not muster the resolution to plunder or disperse this elemental part of you. It is as though a freak accident of nature occurred and a vibrant butterfly metamorphosed backwards into its drab caterpillar, leaving behind its luminescent wings, inert and dry. Your raiments have become an irrelevance. Your retreating spirit wafts through your wardrobes, banished by your diminishing physical self.

Up to this point I have hesitated to take the final step that will transform all these elegant garments into piles of cast-offs, superior jumble. Today, determination has finally overcome restraint and I begin by emptying shelves into many boxes and bags. I ask myself why I choose to do it this way when there are people who do this for a living, people who will clear out the lot in half an hour and spirit it all away. I know the answer lies buried somewhere deep amongst anger and grief. I manage only an hour at a time as the heady bouquet of perfume, lingering in your room, fires memories of long ago fragrances when I knew who you were, or believed that I did. In the fifties, when L'Aimant by Coty passed for sophistication, I recall that I saved up my pocket money to buy you the soap or the talc. Now I sit on your bed with your fine clothes festooned around me and memories tumble randomly through my head.

Clothes have been your passion since childhood. You once told me that your father sent off for bundles of exquisite clothes, cast-offs from the rich and advertised in *The Lady* for a pound. Your sense of style was thus conceived. It was nurtured by the products of the woollen mills and silk mills in the town where your father's dealings often led to an unexpected bonus, in the bulky form of a bolt of silk, which he manhandled home on the bus and your mother took straight to the dressmaker, or a sack of fine wool, which she transformed into garments on the thinnest of knitting needles.

After the war you became a woman on a mission to sate a hunger born of deprivation. You would not make a swimsuit from face flannels or a sun top from two scarves, as suggested in *Woman and Home*. Instead, with me trailing reluctantly along, you searched the remnant boxes of Lewis's and Bon Marché for that exclusive piece of fabric with an 'end of roll' label or an almost imperceptible fault. You worked magic with a paper pattern and your ancient sewing machine. Your obsession with exclusivity spurred you on to make what you could not buy. I wouldn't say that you were a follower of fashion except in the broadest sense; lengths, sleeves, necklines, collars, round or pointed? Your real talent lay in your relentless pursuit of quality. "Look at this Gill. Feel that. It is pure wool. This is silk. Feel how cool it is against your skin. Feel the weight. This is sailcloth. It will make a lovely jacket."

Even now, after all these years, I sometimes find myself compressing and rolling fabric between my finger and thumb. You taught me to detect the softness of natural fibres and to root out the resistance in the man-made ones. I learned to inspect seams, check for depth in pockets and the invisibility of zips. It still irks me to be drawn, like a magnet, to clothes I cannot afford, but in spite of your gift of a sewing machine when I was twenty-one I never followed your lead. You gave me all the tools, but I didn't have the passion. You, by this time, had been recreated by providence and your sewing machine went into retirement as your new man indulged your passion. After a brief fling with Marks & Spencer you glided effortlessly into Jaeger, Kendal Milne and House of Fraser. Coty went out through the window, and Nina Ricci and Giorgio Armani moved in. From your self-satisfied heights, you and Peter spent the rest of your lives looking down upon and mocking those you considered less elegant than yourselves.

I don't feel any compassion towards the contents of your wardrobes. They are merely a logistical problem. Your finery is no longer relevant, to you or to me. The woman who wore these clothes retreated years ago. Only her spectre bides its time at Lamont. You never believed in charity. Peter always bandied words like 'scroungers', 'a decent day's work' and 'corruption'. You just echoed his sentiments.

When everything is boxed and bagged I do the same for you as I did for him and make a very generous donation on your behalf to provide some Christmas surprises for the people who regularly trawl for bargains in the shops for Saint Luke, the Red Cross and Cancer Relief.

CHAPTER TWENTY THREE

NOSTALGIA

I ring the bell, sign the book in the porch and squeeze antibacterial gel onto my hands. A smiling Chinese girl is already opening the door.

"Hello, you come see Olga? She is in lounge," she says.

I smile my thanks and make my way past a huge teddy bear with a label round his neck which reads, "Guess my name and I am yours for one pound". A pot full of money and a list of improbable names sit beside him on the hall table. I'll ask you. You are much better at naming bears than I am.

Your favourite chair has a view of the apple tree. On your right is Miriam, who 'la la las' all day long, and on your left is Nellie, who never speaks but is constantly sliding out of her chair despite the carers' best efforts to wedge her in.

You look frail today. Your pallor is accentuated by an angry bruise on the side of your forehead, inflicted by a door that saw you before you saw it. Daniel had already informed me that you had become confused after taking antibiotics for a persistent cough and misjudged the bathroom door.

The Music Man has come this afternoon to pluck the strings of tangled minds and strike the chords of long ago. The carers shuffle everyone up close to make more space in the lounge. It causes consternation.

"What is going on? Please will someone tell me? Please?"

"Are they going to turf us out? I don't want to go. I'm not ready to go today."

"Are we going to say prayers? Is that the Vicar over there?"

"Someone's taken all my clothes! Where have you put my clothes? I can't find them."

"Norman! Are you there? Where's Margie? Is she coming, Norman? Can you get my purse? Norman!"

"Private 9,4,6,7,5,1 sir! I never killed anybody sir. No sir, I did not. Permission to speak, sir!"

The Music Man tunes his guitar, adjusts the sound and begins to sing a medley from your youth. Bing Crosby has come to Lamont to sing especially for you. "Oh, please turn it down la la la," moans Miriam sitting beside you. "It's too loud la la la."

For your deaf ears the level seems just about right. Your faded eyes recover a sparkle. Your fingers begin to tap against the invisible cords holding you in your chair and a wistful smile spreads across your face. You transport yourself back in time and skip down to the Parish Hall wearing your green silk frock and wedge heel shoes. Your flaming hair is Marcel waved, your fair skin rouged and your eyes ablaze.

"You are my sunshine, my only sunshine. You make me happy when skies are grey."

"What d'ya wanna make those eyes at me for if they don't mean what they say?"

"Bring me sunshine, in your smile."

The lyrics hover around your lips, but never quite make a connection. Your feet, laced into your soft leather flats, tap in time with the beat as you whirl and twirl in your head, changing partners with every tune. Your tiny frame in that huge chair shrugs off the mantle of old age and for a brief interlude recaptures the grace and fusion of your youth. The music lifts you, like a long-forgotten marionette from a dusty box. The strings are twisted and some are broken, but the hands and feet still move to the rhythm of the dance.

When the music finally stops you clap your hands above your head. Your eyes are shining now. "Oh, that was lovely. Lovely. I wish I could remember the words. There are so many memories in my head but no words. No one left to share memories with now but I can share them with myself, I can still do that. So I do."

Your eyes and mine brim with tears. The Music Man puts away his box of memories, his cables and guitar and the carers bring in a trolley with the teas. Sandwiches and cakes, fruit jelly and ice cream. The memories fade as quickly as they came and life trundles on.

"Oh do shut that door la, la, la. It's letting in a draught, la, la, la."

"Music? Was there music? In here? I don't remember that."

CHAPTER TWENTY FOUR

TRANSITION

You and I have spent more time together since Peter died than in the whole of the rest of my life, apart from my first five years, of which my recollections are mainly dependent on photographs and hearsay. By all accounts I was a confident and vociferous child, before you sent me to a convent school where the nuns demanded docility and compliance. I was a solitary small person wedged in between you and Bill. I used to long for a brother or sister and ultimately invented a brother for myself, which was fine until my imaginings leaked out of my head and caused a heap of trouble. To account for the fact that no one ever saw this brother of mine, I also had to invent a debilitating condition for him to suffer from. It all fell apart when the mother of one of my school friends was moved to express her sympathy for you. You were appalled by my deceit and I didn't get any pocket money for a long time after that.

As a teenager I was always aware that I wasn't quite doing justice to the role of your imagined daughter. You were unfailingly kind but also always in control, and you were my champion against a dour, unloving father. However, your price was high. You manipulated my ideas and orchestrated my life to suit your own needs. You groomed me and pushed me through any hoops that you thought might lead me to the excitement and glamour you had craved for yourself. Ballroom dancing classes were followed up with tickets for the NSPCC balls which were held in the grand house of the local Marquis. Here, you hoped I would meet the right people. What you didn't seem to understand was that *we* were not the right people, and they didn't particularly want to meet me. 'Mummy' wasn't related to Sir Percy Coulthard. 'Daddy' wasn't a director of something, nor did he work at the BBC. We didn't own a house with grounds and go off to the Alps in the winter to ski. You made me exquisite frocks and I knew how to speak like them, but they soon saw through the facade when they discovered that I really did go to the local school.

Before Peter came back to carry you off in his dark green Wolseley with walnut trim, I was your only ticket out of a disappointing union. You dreamed I'd marry a lawyer, an airline pilot or a captain of industry, but by the time I was sixteen I think you had just about given up on me. I had lost my confidence in my teens; I was an outsider at school because I was English, and an outsider with the English upper crust because I was not quite English enough.

I think I had always been aware of an underlying note of discord between us, but it was many years before the fundamental truth dawned and I understood, that for you, a girl child was second best. The son you had dreamed of before I was born and prematurely named Bruce, had failed to turn up. I recall an afternoon when I took you to an appointment with the psychiatrist and he asked you, "Do you have children?"

"Well, there's a question" you said, and turning to look at me, you replied, "You should know the answer to that one."

I reminded you that the question was not directed towards me and your attention went back to him. With a conspiratorial smile, you said, "I expect you mean boys. Sadly, no boys, but a girl is okay I suppose."

The psychiatrist cast a quizzical look in my direction. I shrugged my shoulders and smiled the smile I had learned to smile to hide the ache inside.

You have been at Lamont for a year and a half. You have no idea where you are, but they are kind and you are warm and comfortable. You have your hair done once a fortnight and the same person does your nails. The chiropodist comes to attend to your feet, but you still refuse to see the dentist. Various activities keep you amused and there is even an occasional trip to the local theatre.

"It was a stroke of luck my finding this place and Peter's very fond of it too," you say. "Nothing is too much trouble for them. I don't think I've received a bill yet though. I must check up on that."

"No need to worry" I say. "I think it's all taken care of."

"Do you think so? I'm not so sure about that."

When I talk to friends about you, they always ask the same question. "Does she still recognise you?" It is the scenario everyone dreads. A much-loved spouse, mother or father disappears to a far-away place behind their eyes, and families fall apart. You, however, have invented a particular brand of discomfort to dispense. We are already strangers by default and I have become accustomed to the inevitability of your complete retreat at some point in the future. I have imagined a gradual fading with ever more missing pieces in the jigsaw of our lives. Bill is long gone. Peter is gone. The grandchildren and great-grandchildren flit around your head without names, ages or birthdays, stuck in their infancy while they plough on through their teenage years.

The Mistress of Memory regularly calls up your mum, your dad and your sister for a chat. Your childhood home is in the forefront of your mind. You point to the lights on the wall in the lounge where we sit. "Auntie Maud and I chose those wall lights, you know, when Ma and Pa were away one time. Ma never liked them, but they are still here."

Today I am thrown into confusion by an unexpected twist. All those hours alone in your head, all the jumbled thoughts, have finally produced a sweeter scenario, one that doesn't leave such a bitter flavour on your tongue. Your skill at writing scripts has not deserted you yet. You have conjured up a replacement daughter, more like the one you yearned for than the one who sits here each week. For the first time since I have been coming to visit, you don't smile or raise your hands in greeting as I enter the room. I am just another visitor.

"Oh, have you come to see me? That's lovely, would you like to sit down? I'm sure they will find you a chair if you ask."

A nurse brings a pot of coffee on a tray, as she does each week. You admire the china cups and declare it is "the best cup of tea you have had all day". You go on, "They seem to know you quite well here. Do you pop in often?"

"I come to see you every week."

"Do you really? Well, there's a thing. And what about your little ones? Are they having a good time? What about Daddy? Have you seen him lately?"

Whose daddy, I wonder – yours? Mine? The grandchildren's or the great grandchildren's? Too many daddies rolled into one. I simplify things.

"He's fine."

"Gill's gone to the States. Did you know? Going to be away for several months I think, She's sorting out some financial deal with the company over there and she'll be meeting up with my son Bruce, I expect. Of course he's a wizard with figures. Peter relies on him."

While I am recovering my composure, you launch into a tale of Gill's two boys. A pair of rascals, by all accounts. "So much energy and such fun. Have you met them? No? They play with Vera's two boys quite a lot, always up and down the lane and across the fields."

There seems no point in saying that if Vera were alive she would be a hundred and two, and she only had a daughter, as did you. I had thought it would be fairly straightforward to be written out of your script, having never really played a significant part, but the convolution of your rewrite has me flummoxed. My life, my career and my daughters are not just erased but replaced by fictional characters whom you find more satisfying. Discussion is no longer an option, much less remonstration. You don't disagree with the demented. You have relocated the book of my life from Non Fiction and into Fiction, and you have won again.

CHAPTER TWENTY FIVE

DISCONNECTION

It is the day of the Summer Fete at Lamont. Since early morning, activities have been underway to transform the medium-sized, rather formal garden. A marquee has been set up. Flags wave above its open portals and flutter in sweeping arcs from tree to tree around the lawn. It is getting close to opening time and a stream of carers are carrying easy chairs outside and placing them around the periphery of the marquee. The Music Man has already set up his sound system and is broadcasting Cliff Richard's *Summer Holiday* and *Living Doll*, interspersed with tunes from the Glenn Miller Orchestra. Friends and relatives, erecting tables in sheltered spots around the garden, cast anxious glances towards the sky.

"Don't worry" Daniel Lamont tells them confidently. "In all the years we've been doing this, we have never had rain."

The carers are now shepherding residents towards the marquee. It is an excruciatingly slow procession. You are all warmly wrapped against the searching chill of an English summer breeze. When you are finally settled, the girls tuck blankets around your knees and feet. Several of them keep watch and reassure while you adjust to your new surroundings.

Private 9,4,6,7,5,l is pushed into the marquee in his wheelchair. "Put the light out! Don't shine the light! I didn't kill anyone. I did not!"

Next comes Miriam, "Oh dear! It's much too cold la la la! Put a bit more coal on the fire la la la!"

Lastly, they bring May, worrying as usual. "When's Margie coming, Norman? Norman, are you there? Where's Margie? Did you tell her, Norman?"

As two o'clock approaches, the nurses bring out a table laden with raffle prizes. Daniel takes off his white coat and becomes Master of Ceremonies, using the Music Man's microphone. He is thanking everyone for their efforts when the sun finally breaks through. The Music Man kicks off with *The Sun Has Got His Hat On* and the crowd cheers. My daughters, Rebecca and Bronwen, and your great-granddaughters, Molly and Lidia, are with me today. In the days before dementia you would probably have made a flippant remark about all girls together, but as you receive their hugs and smiles, I know they have become strangers locked in your past and I wonder how each will react to being erased from your memory.

Rebecca plants a kiss on your papery cheek and stands back, hesitant, then draws her daughter forward.

"This is Molly. You haven't seen her for a little while."

"Hello Molly. Oh, I expect you hate that hair. I hated mine.

Do they call you Ginger?"

Molly looks to her mum for guidance. Bronwen dives in to the rescue; ever the more direct of my two daughters. "Hello Olga. I'm Bronwen. I've come from Spain to see you and I've brought Lidia to say hello."

"That's very kind of you. I think we had a Bronwen once, but she was not as big as you. Just a little girl still at school. A bit like this one, really."

You point at Lidia, who is completely overwhelmed by meeting an old woman she has seen only in photographs. Bronwen laughs and kisses your cheek. "Shall we go for a little walk? You can show us the garden."

The two young women take an arm each and slowly you stroll from stall to stall. All the usual things are there; books and CDs, white elephants and bric-à-brac, home-made cakes, jams and jellies. The toy stall is piled high with orphan teddies, boxes of Lego and games. Of course there is nothing you require, but shopping used to be one of your joys in life.

"Here's your purse Mum," I say. I hand you one I have brought with me, primed with pound coins for you to spend.

"I think this used to be one of Ma's" you say, looking at it closely, but you show no interest in doing any shopping. You used to love the market stalls and if there was a bargain to be had you would always find it. It was something Peter never understood about you. He would steer you into Bratt and Evans to buy a Windsmoor outfit and a couple of days later you'd find a matching jumper on a stall selling designer cast-offs in your local market.

Rebecca and Bronwen take the little ones now to spend their pocket money and play the tombola. You and I stroll slowly among the milling crowd. We stop to watch one of the nurses being pelted with wet sponges in the stocks. You had rolled up your sleeves a year ago and had scored a couple of hits. I'd had no idea you could throw. You had examined all the goods for sale and bought yourself a teddy bear because he had 'such a lovely face'. Now there is a sense of fragility around you, as though you are floating between this garden and some other place; your feet hardly in touch with the ground.

We make our way to the terrace overlooking the garden where Rebecca and Bronwen are deep into catch-up talk and the two little ones are concentrating on ice cream cones, each wanting to be the last to finish, before skipping off for yet another go on the tombola. We sit down for cups of tea and scones. Daniel Lamont dances a waltz on the grass with one of the residents, as the Music Man sings "Lonely rivers flow, to the sea, to the sea. Lonely rivers sigh, wait for me…"

Molly and Lidia rush back to show you their prizes; a yellow dinosaur and a dragon with a vibrating tail. The raffle is drawn, and I win a bottle of brandy. We ask a young nurse to take a photograph of us, all girls together. Then the girls take their daughters for a final look round to spend what is left of their money. They buy cake and raspberries for old time's sake and pots of strawberry jam. You and I sit quietly on the terrace before I walk with you back to your chair in the marquee.

"Have you enjoyed it?" I ask.

"Oh yes. I love this place, don't you? And I'm sure that if Gill were here, she would like it too."

CHAPTER TWENTY SIX

CONCLUSION

I have contemplated your death. Of course I have. Several likely scenarios have played in my head; a fall, a fractured hip or leg, your final days spent in a geriatric ward; a stroke perhaps, followed by long vigils at your bedside; a stubborn infection that refused to succumb to the magic of antibiotics, or perhaps a more gentle fading, dementia claiming your voice, your mobility, your appetite, by slow degrees.

I have, inevitably I suppose, also speculated on my own reaction to your departure. Will it trigger the release of a tide of suppressed grief? Will my stoical self shut everything down and let me ride the wave? I had a dream in which I held your bird-light frame and whispered, "I forgive you," just before you died. The image stayed with me for days while I struggled with the notion that we really should forgive each other. It is not something I would ever expect from you, but I remain an unknown quantity, even to myself.

You have no perceivable ailments on which to base any assumptions, although I know that the situation could change in an instant. At ninety-three you are frail but nimble, cheerful and content; standing securely in line for your birthday greeting from the Queen. You are stone deaf, but you are still making people laugh and laughing with them. You don't know me from Adam and we start afresh each week.

It is with reasonable confidence, then, that I arrange to go and see Bronwen in Spain for a few days in the autumn. I visit you the day before I leave. I take you a soft apple-green fleece. If you like it, I will buy you some more to keep you cosy through the dark days of winter. You pat it gently as if it were a living thing. You hold its softness approvingly against your cheek. Then you hand it back with a smile, unable to grasp that I've brought it for you.

The usual tray of coffee arrives for us to share. You remark on the beautiful blue sky and the abundance of apples on the tree outside the window, then you continue to fasten and unfasten the buttons on your cardigan with painstaking concentration.

"Have I got it right now? I try to be a good girl and get them right. I don't want to be shouted at."

I assure you they are in good order and you begin unfastening them again. You are too preoccupied by the buttons to engage in conversation today, so I sit quietly observing you. I remember when your fingers were agile, flying across four needles, turning heels and shaping toes, never referring to any pattern. I remember the animated conversations we had over the clues to cryptic crosswords, to compensate for ones we should have had about real things, but never did. I look around the room full of folk who have been lifted out of their real lives and set down to wait in limbo. They are being fed with spoons and cups with spouts. They fret about buttons or misdemeanours from their past. They talk to people who are never there to answer their questions and fall away into silence when their visitors come because they don't recognise them any more.

We drain the last drops from the coffee pot. You remind me again that the cups belong to your mother, so I must be careful with them and I stand up to take my leave.

"I'm going to see Bronwen for a few days, but I'll be over to see you when I get back. I'll bring you something special from Spain."

The information doesn't register. The buttons command your attention again. I kiss your cool cheek and my lips sense the bony form beneath. When I reach the doorway of the lounge. I turn to wave as I usually do, no longer expecting a reciprocal gesture. On this particular occasion you look up from the task in hand and call out, "Take care". Five days later the telephone rings in Spain and the circle is complete. There is a tap on my door. The light in the hall throws my daughter into shadow as she approaches my bed holding a mug of tea. It is early morning. She is not yet dressed.

"I'm so sorry Mum, but Dad's just rung to say Olga died in the night."

Death crept into Lamont while my back was turned and you left with him without a protest or a fight. I release a sigh that I have held for a lifetime as this dear girl holds my hand and strokes my face. The silence grows between us.

"Are you okay?" she asks. "is there anything I can do for you… get for you?"

I nod and then shake my head. My mind is in disarray. I want to shout, "You didn't wait to say goodbye!" But then I think, why would you? No use now for an apple-green fleece. Your delicate hands will be frozen before the end of the day. No more trays of coffee disguised as tea. No tears fall but no words form either. It's over.

I ponder on life's peculiar symmetry. This is where it began, with the message about Peter imparted on the same Spanish phone. Did you spare me a frantic dash home to say goodbye or deny me one last time? *"What does it have to do with her?"* Reason corrects me, reminds me that you moved far beyond any rational thought a long time ago. Yet you died, as you had lived, at a distance. Your final moments were shared with someone else's daughters, who loved you in their professional way.

When I return to Lamont a few days later to collect your few possessions, Daniel sits me down in the office with a cup of coffee. He is shocked, he says. They all are. Then he tells me, "We loved your mum. She treated everyone with respect. She was so caring and so kind. She made us laugh. You know, she was a real lady. Everybody loved her."

This, finally, makes me weep. Not so much from a sense of loss as from regret that we were such an ill-matched pair, each of us loved in our separate worlds and each so disappointed by the other. I suspect that grief may come later, when the past loosens its grip. Time is even now smoothing the edges of resentment and revealing that I, mistakenly, believed the discord between us was all about you. I now accept that it was, indisputably, at least as much about me.